By GEORGE E. ROSS

Illustrated by
Seymour Fleishman

KNOW YOUR

DECLARATION
OF INDEPENDENCE

and *THE 56 SIGNERS*

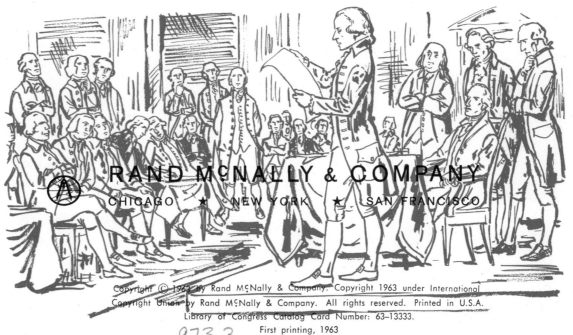

RAND McNALLY & COMPANY
CHICAGO ★ NEW YORK ★ SAN FRANCISCO

CONTENTS

PART TWO

I HAVE never had a feeling, politically, that did not spring from the sentiments embodied in the Declaration of Independence. I have often pondered over the dangers which were incurred by the men who assembled here, and framed and adopted that Declaration of Independence. I have pondered over the toils that were endured by the officers and soldiers of the army who achieved that independence. I have often inquired of myself what great principle or idea it was that kept this confederacy so long together. It was not the mere matter of the separation of the colonies from the motherland, but that sentiment in the Declaration of Independence which gave liberty, not alone to the people of this country, but, I hope, to the world, for all future time.

ABRAHAM LINCOLN
*Speech delivered at
Independence Hall, Philadelphia,
February 21, 1861.*

PART One

THE STORY OF

THE DECLARATION

OF INDEPENDENCE

EACH year, on the Fourth of July, we celebrate the birthday of the United States. With parades, and speeches, and fireworks displays, Americans everywhere show their pride in and their love for their country. This is the day that brings all Americans closer together, and we remember the story of how, in 1776, our country became a nation.

When we celebrate the Fourth of July we are not celebrating the beginning of the Revolutionary War. That happened a year earlier, when, on April 19, 1775, the British troops first clashed with the American Minute Men at Lexington and Concord. Nor are we celebrating the victorious end of the Revolution. That was not to come until 1782, after six years of hard and bitter fighting.

What we do celebrate on this day is the event that took place on July 4, 1776, at the State House in Philadelphia, when a group of patriotic and determined men made the momentous decision to issue a *Declaration of Independence*. "The Glorious Fourth" is our national birthday because it marks the date when the thirteen colonies declared their independence from Great Britain and became a new nation—the United States of America. This was the turning point in our history. From now forward the colonists were Americans, not Englishmen, and the future of their country was in their own hands.

HOW OUR NATIONAL BIRTHDAY BEGAN

The decision to break away from Great Britain was not made hastily. In fact, up until the early part of 1776, most colonists still considered themselves loyal to the Crown, even though they were opposed to the rule of Parliament and the king's ministers.

For many years, however, the tide of events leading toward the Declaration had been gathering momentum. To find the beginning we would have to go back a long way—perhaps to the very founding of the colonies. From the first, the colonists had had to depend largely on their own efforts for survival in the New World. They had become hardy, self-reliant, and impatient of any outside interference or control. Also, the colonies had always had considerable freedom in governing themselves through their town meetings and provincial assemblies, and they came to resent more and more any interference or dictation from the royal governors who represented the Crown. Conflicts between the assemblies and the royal governors were nothing new, but up until about 1760 the colonists were reasonably contented with their treatment by the British government.

Then in 1760 George III came to the throne, determined to take the reins of government into his own hands. He believed that the king should really rule, and he constantly used his influence to get Parliament to act as he wanted. Further, George III was stubborn and autocratic by nature, and resented any opposition to his will either in Parliament or in the colonies. This attitude, naturally, did nothing to help matters when disputes arose with the colonists. His policies and wishes were supported in Parliament by a group of men known as the "King's friends."

TAXATION WITHOUT REPRESENTATION

In 1763 the French and Indian War (called the Seven Years' War in Europe) came to an end, with important results for the American colonies. The defeat of the French meant that the colonists did not have to fear attacks from Canada any more, and hence they were not so dependent on Great Britain

for military protection. But the British government, needing to raise money to pay the costs of the war, now passed several acts designed to bring in more revenue from the colonies. First, they called for a strict enforcement of the earlier Navigation Acts, which regulated colonial trade. This caused the colonial merchants to grumble, though they admitted it was legal. But a real storm of protest broke in 1764–65 when Prime Minister Grenville called for a Stamp Tax—the payment of a small fee on all legal documents—as a means of raising money to help pay the expenses of British troops which were to be garrisoned in the colonies. The colonists were accustomed to taxing themselves, but this was the first time that Parliament had ever levied a direct tax on them. Immediately they protested that such a tax was illegal because they had no representatives in Parliament. It was "taxation without representation." It had long been an accepted principle of English law that the people could be taxed only through their representatives, and the colonists, as Englishmen, claimed this right, too. Further, they had never requested and did not want garrisons of British troops.

THE STAMP ACT CONGRESS

Throughout the colonies there were indignant meetings to protest the Stamp Act, and in Boston and elsewhere mobs rioted and threatened the men appointed to collect the tax. Patriot groups called "Sons of Liberty" pledged themselves not to buy British goods. On May 29, 1765, the Virginia Assembly (or House of Burgesses), fired by a speech by Patrick Henry, passed a resolution declaring that only the Assembly had the right to levy taxes on the inhabitants of Virginia. On June 8, Massachusetts proposed that the colonies send delegates to a convention to draw up a "general and united" protest to the king and Parliament. This convention—known as the Stamp Act Congress—met in New York on October 7. Delegates from nine colonies were present, including such highly respected leaders as James Otis and Robert Livingston of New York, and John

Dickinson of Pennsylvania. After two weeks of debate they drew up a "Declaration of Rights and Grievances of the Colonists in America," in which they respectfully insisted that they could not be legally taxed by the British Parliament.

As a result of these protests, which were supported by William Pitt and other Parliamentary leaders opposing the "King's friends," the Stamp Act was repealed in 1766. At the same time, however, Parliament declared that the colonies were "subordinate unto and dependent upon" Great Britain, and that Parliament had full power to make laws governing them.

THE TOWNSHEND ACTS

A year after the repeal of the Stamp Tax, a new Chancellor of the Exchequer, Charles Townshend, proposed another means of raising money from the colonies. The "Townshend Acts" of 1767, as they were called, required the payment of import duties on certain articles the colonists had to buy from Great Britain, such as tea, paper, colors, and glass. Townshend claimed this was a regulation of commerce, not an "internal tax," but the colonial leaders refused to accept his argument. They saw clearly that these duties were simply another form of taxation.

Leaders among the colonists once more called for resolutions of protest through the colonial assemblies. In February, 1768, Massachusetts sent out a circular letter declaring

the new acts unconstitutional, and invited the colonies to make another united protest to Parliament. The British government, angered by this opposition, directed the royal governors to dissolve the colonial assemblies if they attempted to pass such resolutions. It also proposed to send American agitators to England for trial, and dispatched troops to Boston to keep order.

Although the collection of the import duties was enforced, the British government soon found that the cost of enforcement was greater than the amount collected. Throughout the colonies, "non-importation agreements" were voted and enforced by the patriots. In April, 1770, therefore, all the Townshend duties were repealed, except for the tax on tea, which was left to assert Parliament's authority—and the king's.

THE BOSTON MASSACRE

After the repeal of the Townshend Acts, tension eased in the colonies—except in Boston, where there was constant friction between the citizens and the garrison of British troops. On March 5, 1770, a squad of soldiers, goaded by the taunts of a rowdy mob, had fired into the crowd and killed five persons. This incident was immediately labeled "the Boston Massacre," and caused great indignation throughout the colonies. As a result of public protests, the troops were finally withdrawn from Boston and the accused men tried for manslaughter. It is inter-

esting to note that they were defended by John Adams and Josiah Quincy, and that all but two were acquitted.

COMMITTEES OF CORRESPONDENCE

Although the majority of colonists, perhaps, were still willing to renew friendly relations with Great Britain, there was a growing number of more ardent patriots who were already looking forward to complete independence. Chief of these was Samuel Adams of Boston, a natural-born agitator, who threw himself heart and soul into the work of keeping up the spirit of resistance. Through his efforts, "Committees of Correspondence" were organized in principal towns throughout Massachusetts and later throughout the colonies, which helped to spread the arguments for independence among the people. This network of hard-working patriots formed an organization which was to play an important part in later events. It was, in fact, the beginning of a real union of the colonies.

THE BOSTON TEA PARTY—1773

Although Parliament had repealed the hated Townshend Acts (except for the duty on tea), King George and his ministers continued to interfere in the internal affairs of the colonies in various ways. Enforcement of the Navigation Acts hampered the growing trade of the colonies. The provincial assemblies were dissolved or ignored by the royal governors; local officers were appointed who were to be paid by the Crown instead of by the colonies.

These arbitrary acts irritated and alarmed the colonists, but they did not become fully aroused until in 1773 King George tried to force the colonies to accept shipments of tea from the East India Company, which was in financial difficulties. The tea was priced cheaply and the import duty was slight, but the colonists saw this move as still another attempt to tax them without their consent.

From Maine to Georgia the colonies spoke out in angry protest. Public opinion forced many merchants to refuse the shipments of tea. At some ports the tea ships were turned back; at others the tea was unloaded but not sold. In Boston the situation became tense when three ships entered the harbor and Governor Hutchinson insisted that the tea must be landed, even after the town council had refused to accept it. Determined to prevent the landing, some fifty men, disguised as Indians, boarded the ships on the night of December 16, 1773, and threw 342 chests of tea into the salt waters of Boston Harbor.

THE "INTOLERABLE ACTS"

This act was hailed throughout the colonies as a heroic defense of colonial liberties, but the king's ministers regarded it as a lawless riot. Lord North, the Prime Minister, decided that Boston must be taught a lesson, and he put through Parliament five measures which became known as the "Intolerable Acts." The Port of Boston was to be closed

to all trade in order to starve the citizens into submission; town meetings were restricted and power concentrated in the hands of the royal governor; soldiers were to be quartered on the citizens, and any British officers or men accused under civil law were to be tried in England. In addition, the Ohio region claimed by Connecticut, Massachusetts, and Virginia was to be annexed instead to the Quebec territory. A few weeks later, General Gage arrived in Boston to act as governor and to enforce the decrees.

THE FIRST CONTINENTAL CONGRESS

This harsh treatment of Boston aroused the sympathies of the other colonies and united them behind her. When Samuel Adams proposed that a colonial convention or congress be called to meet in Philadelphia and discuss the situation, some of the most influential men in America came as delegates—men like George Washington and Patrick Henry from Virginia, John Jay from New York, John Adams from Massachusetts, and John Dickinson from Pennsylvania. All the colonies except remote Georgia were represented.

This was the First Continental Congress. It met September 5, 1774, and remained in session until October 26. Its chief work was to prepare a "Declaration of Rights" for the colonies, stating their grievances against the British government. This declaration did not call for independence; it simply claimed for the colonists the same rights and privileges that were enjoyed by other British subjects. The Congress also voted that if these grievances were not corrected, a second Congress should meet in May, 1775. In the meantime, the delegates united in an "Association" pledged not to import goods from England.

LEXINGTON AND CONCORD

During the next six months matters grew steadily worse. King George and his ministers, although disturbed by the course events were taking in America, refused to make any important concessions. They did not believe that the colonies could ever form a united front, or that they would dare risk a war with Great Britain. But American tempers

were rising. When the royal governors tried to dissolve the provincial assemblies, others were organized secretly. "Committees of Safety" were formed to carry on the business of government. In Virginia, Patrick Henry made his fiery "Give me liberty or give me death" speech. In Massachusetts, the citizens, defying General Gage, were already beginning to gather arms and were preparing to raise a military force.

Gage received orders from London to arrest Samuel Adams and John Hancock as the ringleaders, and on April 18, 1775, he sent troops to Lexington, Massachusetts, to seize the two patriots and also to destroy the military stores there. But the alarm was given by Paul Revere on his famous ride; Adams and Hancock escaped, and when the British troops reached Lexington they found a body of Minute Men drawn up on the green to oppose them. Here the first shots of the Revolution were fired, and several of the Minute Men were killed. The British proceeded to Concord, but were forced to retreat to Boston, pursued by increasing numbers of colonial sharpshooters. The British lost 273 men; the Americans 93.

THE SECOND CONTINENTAL CONGRESS

When the Second Continental Congress met in May, 1775, some members still hoped that peace could be restored without a final break between the colonies and Great Britain.

There was a strong Loyalist sentiment in several of the colonies and a feeling that the king was being misled by his ministers. At the urging of John Dickinson of Pennsylvania, a final petition—known as the "Olive Branch" petition—was prepared and sent to England on July 8. But at the same time, the Congress was recommending that a Continental Army be organized, and George Washington of Virginia was appointed as Commander-in-Chief. A "Declaration of the Causes and Necessity for Taking Arms," was issued, stating: *"The arms we have been compelled by our enemies to assume, we will employ for the preservation of our liberties, being with one mind resolved to die freemen rather than live like slaves."* On June 17, another battle took place outside of Boston, the Battle of Bunker Hill. The British won the fight, but the colonists proved once more that they could stand up against regular troops.

The "Olive Branch" petition was rejected by the British government; in fact, on the day it was delivered, George III issued a proclamation declaring that the colonies were in open rebellion. Meanwhile, the Continental Congress was taking over more and more of the powers of government. It ordered a Continental currency to be issued, and opened American ports to foreign trade.

Events were now moving toward a crisis. On December 6, 1775, the Continental Congress renounced allegiance to the British Parliament, though even yet it professed loyalty to King George. But on December 22 another Royal Proclamation forbade all trade with the colonies and authorized the seizure of American ships. The Revolution was now a fact, even though neither side had formally declared war.

TOM PAINE'S "COMMON SENSE"

The lingering feeling of loyalty to the Crown, still held by many Americans all during 1775, received its death blow with the publication early in 1776 of a small pamphlet called *Common Sense*, by the British writer, Thomas Paine. Paine, who had come to America and taken up the cause of the colonists, made a blistering attack on the whole institution of monarchy and the British monarchy in particular, and called for the colonies to assert their independence. His pamphlet was read and quoted throughout the colonies; over 150,000 copies were sold in one year, and it had a profound effect on public opinion.

All men, (wrote Paine) *whether in England or America, confess that a separation between the countries will take place one time or another. To find out the very time, we need not go far, for the time hath found us. . . . There is something absurd in supposing a continent perpetually governed by an island. . . . A government of our own is our natural right. . . .*

Another factor in hardening the opposition to the king as well as to Parliament was the fact that George III had authorized the hiring of foreign mercenary troops—the

Hessians—to fight against the colonists. By the middle of May, most of the colonies had notified the Congress that they were ready to favor a declaration of independence from Great Britain. On May 15, 1776, the Congress passed a resolution recommending that the colonies form independent governments for themselves.

THE VIRGINIA RESOLUTION

On June 7, Richard Henry Lee of Virginia, acting on instructions received from the Virginia convention at Williamsburg, presented to Congress the following resolution, stating:

That these United Colonies are, and of right ought to be, free and independent States, that they are absolved from all allegiance to the British Crown, and that all political connection between them and the State of Great Britain is, and ought to be, totally dissolved.

That it is expedient forthwith to take the most effectual measures for forming foreign Alliances.

That a plan of confederation be prepared and transmitted to the respective Colonies for their consideration and approbation.

This resolution, which called for a Declaration of Independence and the setting up of a new government for the colonies, was vigorously debated for two days. Nine of the colonies were ready to vote in favor of it, but New York, Pennsylvania, Delaware, and South Carolina still hesitated. Some of the more cautious delegates were still reluctant to break away from Great Britain, at least until they had organized a new government. Others, who personally favored the vote, could not go against the instructions from their legislatures. Further consideration was put off until July 1 to allow the delegates from these colonies time to get fresh instructions from their legislatures. In the meantime, a committee was appointed to draw up the declaration, so that it would be ready when the Virginia Resolution was adopted— as everyone felt confident it would be.

WRITING THE DECLARATION

The committee appointed to draft the Declaration of Independence was made up of Benjamin Franklin of Pennsylvania, Robert Livingston of New York, John Adams of Massachusetts, Roger Sherman of Connecticut, and Thomas Jefferson of Virginia. It was Jefferson who was assigned to draft the wording. There is a story that Jefferson suggested that John Adams, so much better known, should do this, and that Adams refused, giving his reason as follows: "Reason first—You are a Virginian, and a Virginian ought to appear at the head of this business. Reason second—I am obnoxious, suspected, and unpopular. You are very much otherwise. Reason third—you can write ten times better than I can."

At any rate, Jefferson accepted the task and wrote out the draft in longhand in the parlor of the house where he was staying, using a portable writing desk of his own design. He stated later that he used no other books or documents in writing this draft, but undoubtedly his mind was filled with the thoughts and arguments that men had been discussing for months. His own purpose, as he himself said later, was "to place before mankind the common sense of the subject" and to make his document "an expression of the American mind."

Jefferson completed his "rough draft" sometime before June 28, and showed it to

Franklin and John Adams, who made a few minor changes in the wording. The other members of the committee approved this draft, and it was then put aside until Congress resumed its debate on the Virginia Resolution on July 1. By this time the four doubtful colonies were swinging in favor of the majority. The South Carolina delegates had agreed to vote for the resolution. Two conservative members of the Pennsylvania delegation stayed away from the meeting, which left a majority in favor of independence. The Delaware delegates were still evenly divided, and the deciding vote in favor of independence was cast by Caesar Rodney, who rode eighty miles on horseback through a storm to arrive in time to break the tie. The New York delegates still had received no official instructions and so did not vote at all.

Thus, on July 2, 1776, the vote for declaring independence was carried by twelve of the thirteen colonies. John Adams wrote jubilantly to his wife the next day:

Yesterday the greatest question was decided which ever was debated in America, and a greater perhaps never was nor will be decided among men. . . . The second day of July, 1776, will be the most memorable epoch in the history of America. I am apt to believe it will be celebrated in the succeeding generations as the great Anniversary Festival.

He might almost have had a vision of the future! And in a sense, July 2 can truly be called our Independence Day, for it was this vote in favor of the Virginia Resolution that made possible the Declaration.

DEBATING THE DECLARATION

The next day, July 3, was spent in reading and discussing the text of the Declaration that Jefferson had prepared. The text of this "rough draft" is still in existence, and shows the corrections entered in Jefferson's own handwriting. Some of these were his own changes, some had probably been suggested earlier by Franklin and Adams, and some

were made by members of the Congress during the debate on July 3. Most were simply matters of wording, not of the ideas that Jefferson had so eloquently expressed.

It was John Adams who vigorously defended and explained the text of the Declaration during this discussion. Jefferson took no part in the debate except to make notes of the changes voted on his rough draft. Later Jefferson described Adams as "our Colossus on the floor," and said, ". . . his arguments came out with a power, both of thought and expression, that moved us from our seats." Fifty years later, in 1826, Daniel Webster delivered a speech such as he believed John Adams might have made at this time, filled with all the fiery conviction and eloquence at his command. This speech (see p. 20) is often quoted as if it were actually John Adams' own words.

At last everyone was satisfied. The next day, July 4, the Declaration was adopted by a unanimous vote of the twelve colonies (New York did not vote) and was signed by John Hancock as President of the Congress and Charles Thomson as the Secretary. Congress ordered that it be printed immediately for distribution throughout the states, and it was sent to the printer, John Dunlap, that same night. We do not have the actual copy that was used by the printer, but it is very likely that Jefferson had made a fresh copy from his rough draft to show the changes requested by Congress, and that this was the copy John Hancock signed and which the printer used. Later this handwritten copy seems to have disappeared, and the copy attached to the *Journal* of the Congress is one of the printed copies.

Due probably to the haste with which it was printed, this first printing of the Declaration shows many peculiarities of capitalization and punctuation, but no one was inclined to be critical. By July 5 the copies were ready to be dispatched to the various colonies—or states—to be read to all the citizens of the new nation. On July 8 the Declaration was proclaimed in Philadelphia itself, and it was on that day the famous "Liberty Bell" was rung to bring the citizens

A Declaration by the Representatives of the UNITED STATES OF AMERICA, in General Congress assembled.

When in the course of human events it becomes necessary for one people to dissolve the political bands which have connected them with another, and to assume among the powers of the earth the separate and equal station to which the laws of nature & of nature's god entitle them, a decent respect to the opinions of mankind requires that they should declare the causes which impel them to the separation.

We hold these truths to be self-evident; that all men are created equal, that they are endowed by their creator with equal rights, that from that equal creation they derive rights inherent & inalienable, among these are life, liberty, & the pursuit of happiness; that to secure these rights, governments are instituted among men, deriving their just powers from the consent of the governed; that whenever any form of government becomes destructive of these ends, it is the right of the people to alter or to abolish it, & to institute new government, laying it's foundation on such principles & organising it's powers in such form, as to them shall seem most likely to effect their safety & happiness. prudence indeed will dictate that governments long established should not be changed for light & transient causes: and accordingly all experience hath shewn that mankind are more disposed to suffer while evils are sufferable, than to right themselves by abolishing the forms to which they are accustomed. but when a long train of abuses & usurpations [begun at a distinguished period, &] pursuing invariably the same object, evinces a design to reduce them under absolute Despotism, it is their right, it is their duty, to throw off such government & to provide new guards for their future security. such has been the patient sufferance of these colonies; & such is now the necessity which constrains them to expunge their former systems of government. the history of the present king of Great Britain is a history of unremitting injuries and usurpations, [among which appears no solitary fact to contradict the uniform tenor of the rest, but all have] in direct object the establishment of an absolute tyranny over these states. to prove this, let facts be submitted to a candid world, [for the truth of which we pledge a faith yet unsullied by falsehood]

Facsimile of the first page of Jefferson's draft of the Declaration of Independence, showing corrections.

together. The long-awaited news was hailed with popular rejoicing and the celebration of independence continued all that day and most of the night. Throughout the colonies similar celebrations took place wherever the Declaration was read. There were torch-light processions, "Liberty poles" were set up, cannons fired, and figures of George III or the royal coat of arms thrown down by the jubilant crowds. By the end of August the news had been carried to the farthest corners of the country.

SIGNING THE DECLARATION

We like to picture the signing of the Dec-laration of Independence as taking place on July 4, when it was voted on by Congress, but that is not really the way it happened.

The text of the Declaration that was adopted on July 4, 1776, was signed only by John Hancock and witnessed by Charles Thomson. But on July 19, Congress voted that the Declaration should be "fairly en-grossed on parchment . . . and that the same when engrossed be signed by every member of Congress." It also directed that the title be changed at that time to show that the document was now the unanimous declara-tion of the thirteen states, for New York had finally voted its official approval.

On August 2, the new copy of the Dec-laration, engrossed (that is, written in large letters) on parchment was ready, and on that date the members of Congress who were in Philadelphia gathered around a table in the State House to affix their signa-tures. But during the month that had passed,

some of the delegates who had actually voted for the Declaration had left Philadel-phia, and some new delegates had joined the Congress. Hence, not all of the Signers of the Declaration are the same as those who originally voted for it.

It is interesting to note some of the names that do *not* appear on the Declaration. George Washington's name is not there—he was on active duty with the Army at that time. And Patrick Henry's name is missing too, for he had left the Congress to take up the office of governor of Virginia. Robert Livingstone of New York, though on the com-mittee that drafted the Declaration, did not sign it because he was replaced as a delegate before August 4. For the same reason, the name of John Dickinson of Pennsylvania does not appear. Both men had been re-called by their legislatures.

Many stories have been told about the signing of the Declaration. Some perhaps are not historically true, but we like to think they might have been. John Hancock, for example, is said to have made his signa-ture especially large "so that King George could read it without putting on his specta-cles." Benjamin Franklin, always ready to make a joke, is supposed to have remarked that "We must all hang together, or as-suredly we shall all hang separately."

On January 18, 1777, Congress ordered that a new printing be made of the Declara-tion with the names of the Signers added, and a copy of this was sent to each of the thirteen states.

THE MEANING OF THE DECLARATION

The Declaration of Independence is made up of four parts: (1) the preamble or introduction, which simply states the purpose of the document; (2) a paragraph discussing the purpose and nature of governments, and explaining *why* this declaration is being made; (3) a list of specific charges against King George III, justifying the Declaration; and (4) the formal declaration of independence itself. (See pp. 18–19 for text.)

In 1776 it was the list of charges against King George and the final declaration that the colonies were now free that aroused the people and caused the greatest enthusiasm. But it is the preamble and the following paragraph which really contain the whole spirit of the Revolution. Here Jefferson put into glowing words the feelings and beliefs that had been growing in the colonies for many years:

> *We hold these truths to be self-evident, that all men are created equal, that they are endowed by their Creator with certain unalienable Rights, that among these are Life, Liberty, and the pursuit of Happiness.—That to secure these rights, Governments are instituted among Men, deriving their just Powers from the Consent of the Governed.—That whenever any Form of Government becomes destructive of these Ends, it is the right of the People to alter or to abolish it. . . .*

Jefferson was not, of course, the first or only statesman to hold these views. Very similar expressions can be found in other writings of the times, and in such documents as the Virginia "Bill of Rights," adopted on June 12, 1776. But in Jefferson's words they took on a nobility and beauty that have never ceased to uplift American hearts. This is the part of the Declaration that has so greatly influenced American statesmen ever since, and it is still an inspiration and a challenge to us all.

The list of accusations against King George which makes up the greater part of the document is interesting historically, though these charges have little significance to us now. As we read them, however, we are reminded of the grievances the colonies had endured for so many years: the interference with local self-government by the king's officers; the quartering of troops on civilians; taxes imposed without the consent of the colonies; the cutting off of the trade of the colonies; the tyrannical acts of the king in suspending the charters of the colonies, sending foreign mercenary troops against them, and so on. These grievances were listed in detail to convince not only Americans and Englishmen but also outside nations that this Declaration of Independence was necessary and justified.

Finally we come to the formal declaration of independence itself, and here the text repeats the wording of the Virginia Resolution which Congress had already adopted: *"That these United Colonies are and by right ought to be Free and Independent States . . ."* Then, concluding the document, comes that solemn, resolute sentence: *"And for the support of this Declaration, with a firm reliance on the protection of divine Providence, we mutually pledge to each other our Lives, our Fortunes, and our sacred Honor."*

No American can read that sentence without a thrill of pride.

THE DECLARATION TODAY

The engrossed parchment copy of the Declaration, carrying the signatures of the delegates, is the "official" Declaration of Independence. During the Revolutionary War and the next few years the document, together with other government papers, was moved from place to place as the government itself moved, so that at various times it was in Philadelphia, Baltimore, and New York. When the new capital city of Washington was being built, the Declaration was stored there in the War Office building, where it remained until the British attacked the city in 1814. James Monroe, then Secretary of State, removed the Declaration with other state papers to Leesburg, Virginia, but when Washington was rebuilt the Document was brought back again, this time to the Department of State building.

During all these years the parchment had usually been kept rolled up, and there had been some rubbing and smudging of the signatures in the process of rolling and unrolling. In 1841, Secretary of State Webster had the Declaration framed and hung up in the new Patent Office Building, but this exposure to light and changes of temperature faded the signatures still further. By 1877, the 100th birthday of the Declaration, the condition of the document was causing serious concern, and it was finally removed from public view and locked in a safe, sealed between two plates of glass for greater safety.

After World War I, experts decided that it would be safe to allow the Declaration to be exhibited again if it could be kept under a dim light. The Library of Congress seemed the appropriate lodging place for a document of such supreme national importance, and a special "shrine" was prepared for it there and dedicated in 1924. Here the Declaration remained until the United States entered World War II in 1941; it was then transported under armed guard to the vaults of Fort Knox for safekeeping, together with the text of the Constitution.

When the Declaration was brought back to Washington in 1944, the Bureau of Standards applied new techniques to protecting the precious parchment. It was sealed in insulating glass with a special backing to guard it against changes of temperature, and a new lighting system was installed. Once again it was moved to a new home with impressive ceremonies—this time to the new National Archives building, expressly built to house important historical documents.

Here the Declaration has been given a beautiful and fitting setting or shrine where it is visited each year by thousands of citizens. Now over 185 years old, the faded lettering of the Declaration still glows with patriotic fervor, and its stirring phrases still recall our priceless heritage of freedom.

TABLE OF EVENTS LEADING TO THE DECLARATION

DATE	EVENT	DATE	EVENT

1760 George III becomes king and determines to take a more active part in government affairs.

1763 New colonial policy adopted by Great Britain under Prime Minister Grenville: (1) rigid enforcement of the Navigation Acts, (2) taxation of colonies to help support British garrisons, (3) permanent establishment of British troops in the colonies.

1765 Parliament passes Stamp Act as a means of raising money for partial support of colonial army.

May 29 Virginia Assembly protests against Stamp Act.

June 8 Massachusetts suggests that colonies send delegates to New York to draw up a "general and united" remonstrance to the King.

August Riots in Boston against Stamp Act. Organization of "Sons of Liberty" pledged not to buy British goods.

October 7 Stamp Act Congress meets in New York with delegates from nine colonies.

1766, March 18 Parliament repeals the Stamp Act but asserts the principle that Parliament has the right to make laws binding on the colonies.

1767, June "Townshend Acts" passed, laying import duties on tea, paper, glass, and other commodities.

1768, February Massachusetts sends circular letter to other colonies, inviting concerted protests to Parliament against Townshend Acts.

April English government adopts repressive measures toward colonies: (1) directs governors to dissolve assemblies if they attempt to pass resolutions, (2) dispatches troops to Boston, (3) proposes that American agitators be sent to England for trial.

1770, March 5 British troops fire on mob in Boston—the "Boston Massacre."

April Parliament repeals Townshend Acts, except for tax on tea.

1772, November Samuel Adams proposes "Committees of Correspondence" to help the revolutionary parties in the colonies keep in touch with each other.

1773, May Tea Act gives East India Company virtual monopoly on sale of tea in colonies.

December 16 The Boston Tea Party. Citizens of Boston, disguised as Indians, seize shipment of tea and dump it into Boston Harbor.

1774 Parliament passes five "Intolerable Acts" as punishment for the Boston Tea Party.

May General Gage arrives in Boston to become royal governor.

June 17 General Court of Massachusetts passes a resolution proposing a Continental Congress.

September 5 The First Continental Congress assembles at Philadelphia and issues a "Declaration of Rights." Delegates also pledge that they will import no goods from England.

1775, February People of Massachusetts elect a Provincial Congress in defiance of General Gage and prepare to raise a military force.

March 23 Patrick Henry makes "Give me liberty or death" speech.

April 18–19 British troops sent from Boston to Lexington and Concord to seize military stores. Fighting at Lexington and Concord between troops and Minute Men.

May 10 Second Continental Congress assembles at Philadelphia to act as a center of consultation for the colonies.

June 14 The Congress recommends organization of a Continental Army and appoints George Washington as Commander-in-Chief.

June 17 Battle of Bunker Hill.

June 22 The Congress orders a Continental paper currency to be issued.

July 8 Congress prepares the last formal petition sent to the Crown, the "Olive Branch" petition.

August 23 George III issues a Royal Proclamation declaring the colonies in rebellion.

December 6 Congress renounces allegiance to British Parliament, although asserting loyalty to the King.

December 22 A Royal Proclamation forbids all trade with colonies and authorizes seizure of American ships.

1776, January 9 Publication of Thomas Paine's "Common Sense."

May 15 Congress recommends to the colonies that they form new governments.

June 7 Richard Henry Lee presents Virginia's Resolution that the colonies should be "free and independent" states.

June 8 First debate on the Virginia Resolution; vote postponed until July 1st.

June 10 Committee appointed to draft a declaration of independence. Draft completed by June 28.

July 1–2 Further debate in Congress on the Virginia Resolution.

July 2 Congress votes to proclaim independence from Great Britain.

July 3 Debate in Congress on Jefferson's draft of the Declaration.

July 4 The Declaration of Independence adopted by vote of 12 states.

July 5 Printed copies of Declaration sent off to each state to be proclaimed.

July 8 Declaration read to public in Yard of New State House in Philadelphia.

July 9 Declaration adopted formally by New York, completing roll of 13 states.

August 2 Declaration engrossed on parchment and signed by delegates from all thirteen states.

THE DECLARATION OF INDEPENDENCE

In Congress, July 4, 1776

The Unanimous Declaration Of The Thirteen United States Of America

WHEN, in the course of human events, it becomes necessary for one people to dissolve the political bands which have connected them with another, and to assume among the powers of the earth the separate and equal station to which the laws of nature and of nature's God entitle them, a decent respect to the opinions of mankind requires that they should declare the causes which impel them to the separation.

We hold these truths to be self-evident: That all men are created equal; that they are endowed by their Creator with certain unalienable rights; that among these are life, liberty, and the pursuit of happiness; that, to secure these rights, governments are instituted among men, deriving their just powers from the consent of the governed; that whenever any form of government becomes destructive of these ends, it is the right of the people to alter or to abolish it and to institute new government, laying its foundation on such principles, and organizing its powers in such form, as to them shall seem most likely to effect their safety and happiness. Prudence, indeed, will dictate that governments long established should not be changed for light and transient causes; and, accordingly, all experience hath shown that mankind are more disposed to suffer while evils are sufferable, than to right themselves by abolishing the forms to which they are accustomed. But when a long train of abuses and usurpations, pursuing invariably the same object, evinces a design to reduce them under absolute despotism, it is their right, it is their duty, to throw off such government and to provide new guards for their future security. Such has been the patient sufferance of these colonies; and such is now the necessity which constrains them to alter their former systems of government.

The history of the present King of Great Britain is a history of repeated injuries and usurpations, all having in direct object the establishment of an absolute tyranny over these States. To prove this, let facts be submitted to a candid world:

He has refused his assent to laws, the most wholesome and necessary for the public good.

He has forbidden his Governors to pass laws of immediate and pressing importance, unless suspended in their operation till his assent should be obtained; and, when so suspended, he has utterly neglected to attend to them.

He has refused to pass other laws for the accommodation of large districts of people, unless those people would relinquish the right of representation in the Legislature, a right inestimable to them and formidable to tyrants only.

He has called together legislative bodies at places unusual, uncomfortable, and distant from the depository of their public records, for the sole purpose of fatiguing them into compliance with his measures.

He has dissolved representative Houses repeatedly for opposing with manly firmness his invasions on the rights of people.

He has refused for a long time after such dissolutions to cause others to be elected; whereby the legislative powers, incapable of annihilation, have returned to the people at large for their exercise; the State remaining, in the meantime, exposed to all the dangers of invasions from without and convulsions within.

He has endeavored to prevent the population of these States; for that purpose obstructing the laws for naturalization of foreigners, refusing to pass others to encourage their migration hither, and raising the conditions of new appropriations of lands.

He has obstructed the administration of justice by refusing his assent to laws for establishing judiciary powers.

He has made judges dependent on his will alone for the tenure of their offices and the amount and payment of their salaries.

He has erected a multitude of new offices, and sent hither swarms of officers to harass our people and eat out their substance.

He has kept among us, in times of peace, standing armies, without the consent of our Legislatures.

He has affected to render the military independent of, and superior to, the civil power.

He has combined with others to subject us to a jurisdiction foreign to our Constitution and unacknowledged by our laws, giving his assent to their acts of pretended legislation:

For quartering large bodies of armed troops among us;

For protecting them, by a mock trial, from punishment for any murders which they should commit on the inhabitants of these States;

For cutting off our trade with all parts of the world;

For imposing taxes on us without our consent;

For depriving us, in many cases, of the benefits of trial by jury;

For transporting us beyond seas to be tried for pretended offenses;

For abolishing the free system of English laws in a neighboring province, establishing therein an arbitrary government, and enlarging its boundaries so as to render it at once an example and fit instrument for introducing the same absolute rule into these colonies;

For taking away our charters, abolishing our most valuable laws, and altering fundamentally the forms of our governments;

For suspending our own Legislatures, and declaring themselves invested with power to legislate for us in all cases whatsoever.

He has abdicated government here by declaring us out of his protection and waging war against us.

He has plundered our seas, ravaged our coasts, burnt our towns, and destroyed the lives of our people.

He is at this time transporting large armies of foreign mercenaries to complete the works of death, desolation, and tyranny, already begun with circumstances of cruelty and perfidy scarcely paralleled in the most barbarous ages, and totally unworthy the head of a civilized nation.

He has constrained our fellow citizens, taken captive on the high seas, to bear arms against their country, to become the executioners of their friends and brethren, or to fall themselves by their hands.

He has excited domestic insurrections amongst us, and has endeavored to bring on the inhabitants of our frontiers the merciless Indian savages, whose known rule of warfare is an undistinguished destruction of all ages, sexes, and conditions.

In every stage of these oppressions we have petitioned for redress in the most humble terms: our repeated petitions have been answered only by repeated injury. A prince, whose character is thus marked by every act which may define a tyrant, is unfit to be the ruler of a free people.

Nor have we been wanting in attentions to our British brethren. We have warned them from time to time of attempts by their Legislature to extend an unwarrantable jurisdiction over us. We have reminded them of the circumstances of our emigration and settlement here. We have appealed to their native justice and magnanimity, and we have conjured them by the ties of our common kindred to disavow these usurpations which would inevitably interrupt our connections and correspondence. They, too, have been deaf to the voice of justice and of consanguinity. We must, therefore, acquiesce in the necessity which denounces our separation, and hold them, as we hold the rest of mankind, enemies in war; in peace, friends.

We, Therefore, the Representatives of the United States of America, in General Congress assembled, appealing to the Supreme Judge of the world for the rectitude of our intentions, do, in the name and by the authority of the good people of these colonies, solemnly publish and declare that these United Colonies are, and of right ought to be, **Free and Independent States,** that they are absolved from all allegiance to the British Crown, and that all political connection between them and the State of Great Britain is, and ought to be, totally dissolved; and that as free and independent states they have full power to levy war, conclude peace, contract alliances, establish commerce, and to do all other acts and things which independent States may of right do. And for the support of this declaration, with a firm reliance on the protection of Divine Providence, we mutually pledge to each other our lives, our fortunes, and our sacred honor.

JOHN HANCOCK

NEW HAMPSHIRE
JOSIAH BARTLETT
WM. WHIPPLE
MATTHEW THORNTON

MASSACHUSETTS BAY
SAML. ADAMS
JOHN ADAMS
ROBT. TREAT PAINE
ELBRIDGE GERRY

RHODE ISLAND
STEP. HOPKINS
WILLIAM ELLERY

CONNECTICUT
RODGER SHERMAN
SAM'EL HUNTINGTON
WM. WILLIAMS
OLIVER WOLCOTT

NEW YORK
WM. FLOYD
PHIL. LIVINGSTON
FRANS. LEWIS
LEWIS MORRIS

NEW JERSEY
RICHD. STOCKTON
JNO. WITHERSPOON
FRAS. HOPKINSON
JOHN HART
ABRA. CLARK

PENNSYLVANIA
ROBT. MORRIS
BENJAMIN RUSH
BENJA. FRANKLIN
JOHN MORTON
GEO. CLYMER
JAS. SMITH
GEO. TAYLOR
JAMES WILSON
GEO. ROSS

DELAWARE
CAESAR RODNEY
GEO. READ
THO. M'KEAN

MARYLAND
SAMUEL CHASE
WM. PACA

THOS. STONE
CHARLES CARROLL of Carrolton

VIRGINIA
GEORGE WYTHE
RICHARD HENRY LEE
TH. JEFFERSON
BENJA. HARRISON
THOS. NELSON, JR.
FRANCIS LIGHTFOOT LEE
CARTER BRAXTON

NORTH CAROLINA
WM. HOOPER
JOSEPH HEWES
JOHN PENN

SOUTH CAROLINA
EDWARD RUTLEDGE
THOS. HEYWARD, JUNR
THOMAS LYNCH, JUNR
ARTHUR MIDDLETON

GEORGIA
BUTTON GWINNETT
LYMAN HALL
GEO. WALTON

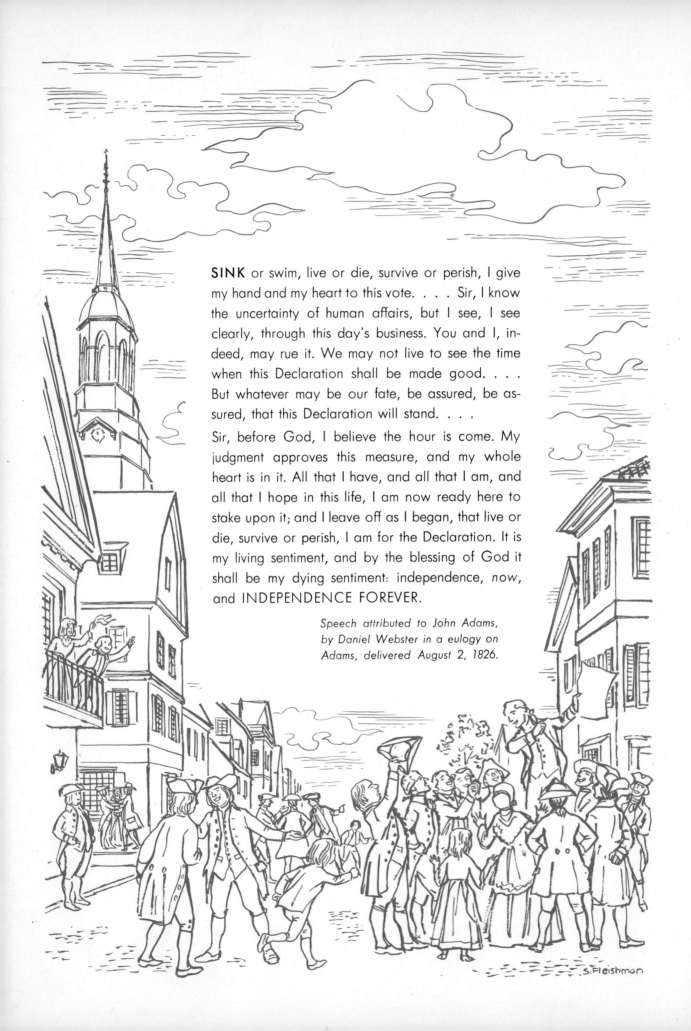

SINK or swim, live or die, survive or perish, I give my hand and my heart to this vote. . . . Sir, I know the uncertainty of human affairs, but I see, I see clearly, through this day's business. You and I, indeed, may rue it. We may not live to see the time when this Declaration shall be made good. . . . But whatever may be our fate, be assured, be assured, that this Declaration will stand. . . .

Sir, before God, I believe the hour is come. My judgment approves this measure, and my whole heart is in it. All that I have, and all that I am, and all that I hope in this life, I am now ready here to stake upon it; and I leave off as I began, that live or die, survive or perish, I am for the Declaration. It is my living sentiment, and by the blessing of God it shall be my dying sentiment: independence, *now*, and INDEPENDENCE FOREVER.

Speech attributed to John Adams,
by Daniel Webster in a eulogy on
Adams, delivered August 2, 1826.

PART Two

THE SIGNERS OF
THE DECLARATION
OF INDEPENDENCE

THE fifty-six Patriots who signed the Declaration of Independence were pledging both themselves and their states to the cause of freedom.

It was not customary for all members of the Continental Congress to sign official papers. Usually only the President and the Secretary signed. But in this case, it was felt that the occasion was so important that every member should put his name on record. All knew that in doing so they were literally risking both their lives and their fortunes, but not a man hesitated.

The delegates signed in groups according to their states, beginning with New Hampshire and ending with Georgia. Pennsylvania had the largest number of delegates—nine. Rhode Island had only two.

The backgrounds of the Signers varied widely, and they represented a broad cross-section of colonial life. Some were self-made men of humble beginnings; others came from homes of wealth and culture. All were leaders in their communities, but this leadership was shown in a variety of ways. More than half were lawyers, and almost all had some training in law. But there were also four doctors and one minister, a number of well-to-do merchants, and two who might be called manufacturers. Most of the southern delegates were wealthy plantation owners. Often, too, these men combined several different careers. A doctor might become a judge; a merchant might also be a commander of militia. And all these men were willing to give up their private businesses to serve their country in this time of crisis, not counting the cost.

Most of the Signers were American-born and of British ancestry. In religion, all but Charles Carroll (a Catholic) were Protestant. Their ages ranged from twenty-six and a half years (Edward Rutledge) to seventy (Benjamin Franklin), with the majority in their thirties or forties.

It is rather difficult to compare the education of the Signers to that of our own day. Many taught themselves by reading widely. Others were educated at home by parents or relatives, or by tutors. Some of the more well-to-do took regular academic degrees at colleges such as Harvard or William and Mary, and a number of the southern delegates were educated abroad.

But whatever their origins or backgrounds, these Signers were all dedicated to the cause of liberty. Almost every one suffered financial losses and hardships as a result of their patriotism; many saw their homes burned and their families forced to flee. Their names should be remembered and honored by every American.

JOHN HANCOCK

1ST SIGNER · MASSACHUSETTS

BORN: JAN. 12, 1736/37

BIRTHPLACE:
BRAINTREE, MASS.

EDUCATION:
HARVARD COLLEGE

OCCUPATION: MERCHANT

MARRIED:
DOROTHY QUINCY, 1775

AGE AT SIGNING: 40

DIED: OCT. 8, 1793. AGE, 56

FIRST to sign the Declaration of Independence was the patriot John Hancock, President of the Second Continental Congress and a delegate from the colony of Massachusetts. He had been born there in the town of Braintree (now Quincy), and was the son of a minister. His father having died when he was an infant, John was adopted and brought up by an uncle, who was the wealthiest merchant in Boston. From this uncle John Hancock inherited a large fortune and a fine home on Beacon Hill, as well as his shipping business. He was educated at Harvard College.

Hancock began his political career by joining in the protests against the Stamp Act in 1765. A merchant himself, Hancock resented the British regulations on colonial trade, and he was among the first to propose and adopt non-importation agreements. His bold defense of the colonial cause, and the fact that his own sloop, the *Liberty*, was seized by the British for non-payment of duties, made him a popular hero in Boston. He was elected to the General Court (the Massachusetts legislature) in 1769, and at the time of the Boston Massacre (1770) he was one of the committee appointed to demand the withdrawal of the British troops. In 1774 and 1775 he was president of the Massachusetts provincial congress, elected in defiance of General Gage, and together with Samuel Adams, was one of the boldest leaders in organizing opposition to the British. In fact,

it was partly for the purpose of seizing Hancock and Adams that General Gage sent soldiers to Lexington on April 18, 1775.

When the Second Continental Congress met in Philadelphia in May, 1775, John Hancock was elected president. It was thus his duty and honor to sign the copy of the Declaration of Independence when it was formally accepted by the Congress on July 4, and his large, bold handwriting stands out conspicuously over all the others.

Hancock resigned as president of the Congress in 1777, but continued as a member. He also saw military action in 1778 as commander of the Massachusetts troops who took part in the expedition against the British in Rhode Island. He was elected the first governor of Massachusetts in 1780, and was re-elected to that office eight times.

Tall, handsome, wealthy, and popular, John Hancock was an outstanding public figure throughout his life. He is said to have been vain of his honors, but he was also open-handed and not afraid to risk his life and fortune in the cause of liberty. "Make John Hancock a beggar, if the public good requires it," he said on one occasion.

Hancock married Dorothy Quincy in 1775 and the couple had two children, but unfortunately both died in childhood. John Hancock himself died on October 8, 1793. His fellow-citizens gave him the most impressive public funeral ever held in New England until that time.

JOSIAH BARTLETT
2ND SIGNER · NEW HAMPSHIRE

BORN: NOV. 21, 1729

BIRTHPLACE: AMESBURY, MASS.

EDUCATION:
COMMON SCHOOLS

OCCUPATION: PHYSICIAN

MARRIED:
MARY BARTON, 1754

AGE AT SIGNING: 46

DIED: MAY 19, 1795. AGE, 65

SINCE the signing of the Declaration began with the northernmost state and proceeded south, Dr. Josiah Bartlett of New Hampshire was the first, after John Hancock, to add his name.

The Bartlett family had first settled in Massachusetts in the late seventeenth century, and Josiah was born in Amesbury in 1729. From his boyhood he was determined to become a doctor of medicine. Although lacking a college degree, he secured his medical training by studying under a relative, and then began to practice in Kingston, New Hampshire. His successful use of "Peruvian bark" (quinine) for the treatment of certain diseases quickly established his reputation, and in 1754 he married his cousin, Mary Barton. Twelve children were born of this union.

As an outstanding man in his community, Dr. Bartlett was elected to the New Hampshire assembly as early as 1765. He was even appointed a colonel of militia by the royal governor, but when trouble began to develop between the colonies and England, he unhesitatingly took the side of the colonies and worked actively for independence. He was a member of the important Committee of Correspondence in New Hampshire, and was sent as a delegate to the Second Continental Congress. Here he voted for and signed the Declaration of Independence, "shaking the rafters with his approval."

Bartlett continued to serve in the later sessions of the Congress and in 1776–77 was on the committee that drafted the Articles of Confederation for the new union of states. The fact that he was appointed chief justice of the court of common pleas in New Hampshire, and was later associate justice and then chief justice of the superior courts is a tribute to his honesty and ability. He was influential in securing New Hampshire's approval of the Federal Constitution in 1788, and he was elected the first governor of his state. In 1794 he retired from public life.

Bartlett is described as having been a man of few words, but respected for his intelligence and integrity. He was a tall man with reddish hair, dignified and rather severe in manner. In addition to his life-long interest in public affairs, he was also active in his profession of medicine and was the organizer and first president of the New Hampshire Medical Society.

Josiah Bartlett died in 1795 at the age of sixty-five. A statue of him, unveiled in 1888, stands in the public square of his native town of Amesbury, and his portrait hangs in the state house of Concord, New Hampsire.

WILLIAM WHIPPLE
3RD SIGNER · NEW HAMPSHIRE

BORN: JAN. 14, 1730

BIRTHPLACE: KITTERY, MAINE

EDUCATION:
COMMON SCHOOLS

OCCUPATION: MERCHANT

MARRIED:
CATHARINE MOFFAT

AGE AT SIGNING: 46

DIED: NOV. 10, 1785. AGE, 55

LIKE John Hancock, William Whipple was a merchant, and like him too, was an early and energetic worker for the cause of independence. Born in Kittery, Maine (though Kittery was then a part of Massa-

William Whipple's wife was his cousin, Catherine Moffat. They had only one child, who died in infancy.

MATTHEW THORNTON

4TH SIGNER • NEW HAMPSHIRE

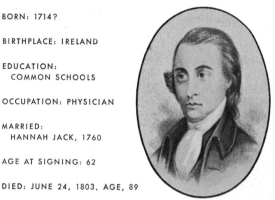

BORN: 1714?

BIRTHPLACE: IRELAND

EDUCATION:
COMMON SCHOOLS

OCCUPATION: PHYSICIAN

MARRIED:
HANNAH JACK, 1760

AGE AT SIGNING: 62

DIED: JUNE 24, 1803. AGE, 89

chusetts), he later moved to Portsmouth, New Hampshire, an active shipping port. Like many boys of his age he went to sea, and while still in his early twenties became master of a ship. In 1760 he returned home, formed a trading company with his brother, and soon became a leading citizen.

Revolutionary sentiment was high among the liberty-loving sailors and traders of Portsmouth, and William won public approval for his bold stand against the British. In 1775 he gave up his share in the trading company to devote his full energy to the colonial cause. As an outstanding patriot, he was elected to the newly organized provincial congress of New Hampshire, and then sent as a delegate to the Second Continental Congress, where he signed the Declaration of Independence and continued to serve until 1779. He also took an active part in the Revolutionary War as a commander of the New Hampshire militia. In fact, he was known as "General Whipple." His letters show that he was a forthright, practical-minded man with strong views and an optimistic disposition. Even when the outlook seemed darkest, he never doubted that the colonies would be victorious.

In the latter years of the war Whipple served on his state legislature, and he was an associate justice of the superior court of New Hampshire from 1782 until his death in 1785.

MATTHEW Thornton was one of the late signers of the Declaration who did not actually vote for it. He was elected to the Second Continental Congress in September of 1776 and did not take his place there until November. Undoubtedly, though, he would have favored the Declaration and would have voted for it.

Matthew Thornton was Irish by birth but Scottish by ancestry. His parents left Ireland to settle in the present state of Maine when he was about four years old. Later they moved to the more settled community of Worcester, Massachusetts, where he attended school. Ambitious to become a doctor, he studied under a Dr. Grout of Leicester, Massachusetts, and then began a successful practice in the town of Londonderry, New Hampshire, where there was a colony of Scots-Irish immigrants.

Dr. Thornton became active in his community as a member of the New Hampshire legislature and adopted the cause of the colonists from the start. He took a prominent part in the protests against the Stamp Tax in New Hampshire, was president of the revolutionary provincial congress set up by the patriot party in 1775, and also acted as chairman of the local Committee of Safety.

When he took his seat in the Continental Congress in November of 1776, Dr. Thornton was sixty-two years old, a very serious-minded man with a naturally grave expression. He remained at the Congress for little more than a year, then returned to New Hampshire where he became an associate justice of the state superior court and later a member of the state senate. One of his most important services was in helping to settle the boundary dispute between New Hampshire and Vermont.

Thornton died in 1803 at the age of eighty-nine and was buried at Merrimack, New Hampshire. The town of Thornton was later named in his honor.

SAMUEL ADAMS

5TH SIGNER • MASSACHUSETTS

BORN: SEPT. 27, 1722

BIRTHPLACE: BOSTON, MASS.

EDUCATION:
HARVARD COLLEGE

OCCUPATION: MERCHANT, POLITICIAN

MARRIED:
ELIZABETH CHECKLEY, 1749
ELIZABETH WELLS, 1764

AGE AT SIGNING: 53

DIED: OCT. 2, 1803. AGE, 81

SAMUEL Adams has been called the firebrand of the Revolution, and certainly no man did more to bring about the American Revolution and the Declaration of Independence. He was one of the first to agitate for separation from England, and he was uncompromising in his demands for complete independence. John Adams, his kinsman, said of Samuel that he was "born and tempered a wedge of steel to split the knot which tied North America to Great Britain."

Adams was born in Boston, a descendant of the Pilgrims. His father was a wealthy deacon of the Old South Church. Samuel was a graduate of Harvard College and also studied law, but gave this up to enter business. Then, failing as a businessman (he had no head for figures), he found his real career in politics. He became known as the leader of the "popular" party, as opposed to the aristocratic ruling class, and was openly critical of British colonial policy. He was one of the leaders in the protests against the Stamp Tax, and as a member of the Massachusetts assembly (1765–1774) took every opportunity to attack the British and to arouse public opinion in Boston against them. The disorders that led to the Boston Massacre may have been—partly at least—the result of his influence, and he undoubtedly took a leading part in planning the Boston Tea Party. He was also a leader in organizing public resistance to the "Intolerable Acts," and as clerk of the assembly corresponded with other colonial leaders to stir up revolutionary sentiment. With Hancock, he was marked for arrest by the British, and only escaped because of the warning given by Paul Revere.

It was Samuel Adams who originated the "Committees of Correspondence" in 1772 to keep the revolutionary groups throughout Massachusetts in touch with each other—an idea that was taken up by the other colonies. It was Adams, too, who urged the colonies to form a Continental Congress for consultation, and he was one of the most active members there. Although not remarkable as an orator, he was persistent and persuasive.

The signing of the Declaration was the high point in Samuel Adams' life. Although he continued to serve in the Continental Congress until the end of the Revolution, and succeeded John Hancock as governor of Massachusetts, his later career cannot match his early years for drama.

Adams had no talent for managing money, and although he inherited a considerable fortune, he eventually lost it all. Most of his adult life was devoted to serving the cause of freedom, for which he received little

financial reward. In fact, when he was elected a delegate to the Continental Congress, his friends had to furnish the money to buy him suitable clothing and a horse. He married twice and had two children, but both died young. Samuel Adams himself died in Boston in 1803, and is buried there in the Old Granary Burying Ground.

JOHN ADAMS
6TH SIGNER · MASSACHUSETTS

BORN: OCT. 30, 1735

BIRTHPLACE:
BRAINTREE, MASS.

EDUCATION:
HARVARD COLLEGE

OCCUPATION: LAWYER

MARRIED:
ABIGAIL SMITH, 1764

AGE AT SIGNING: 40

DIED: JULY 4, 1826. AGE, 90

JOHN Adams, one of the outstanding patriots of the American Revolution and our second President, was a descendant of the John Alden who had been a passenger on the *Mayflower*. Like John Hancock, he was born in Braintree, Massachusetts, and he was a second cousin of Samuel Adams.

After graduating from Harvard College he studied and practiced law, and became noted for his learning and legal ability. He first made his influence felt as a leader of the patriot party in Massachusetts at the time of the Stamp Act protests (1765), when he argued that the Stamp Act was illegal because the colonies had never consented to it. Yet in spite of his support of the colonial cause, Adams showed his moral courage by defending the British soldiers after the Boston Massacre.

Adams was elected to the Massachusetts assembly (the General Court) in 1771, and was sent as a delegate to both the First and the Second Continental Congress. Here he became one of the most influential advocates for independence, impatient of any compromise. He supported the nomination of Washington for Commander in Chief of the Continental forces; he seconded the Virginia Resolution for Independence proposed by Richard Henry Lee; and he was on the committee that drafted the Declaration of Independence. It was Adams, too, who gave the strongest support to the Declaration when it was being debated in Congress (see p. 12). The triumphant letters he wrote to his wife Abigail after the vote show how much the Declaration meant to him.

But the Declaration marked just the beginning of John Adams' long and distinguished career in the service of his country. He later helped draft the constitution of Massachusetts; he served as American Commissioner to France during the war years and was on the committee that negotiated the peace treaty with Great Britain. He was the first American Minister to the Court of George III, served as Vice President under Washington, and succeeded him to the Presidency in 1797.

Adams' term as President was not a happy one. Though acting always for the best interests of the country, he was unpopular with the public because of his stubborn and uncompromising nature. He also quarreled with Thomas Jefferson, his old comrade of Revolutionary days, and left office feeling that his work was unappreciated by the country.

Adams spent his last years in retirement at his home in Braintree, Massachusetts, and he had the satisfaction of seeing his son, John Quincy Adams, elected President in 1824. He was also reconciled with Jeffer-

son, and the two old patriot leaders exchanged many letters. By a strange coincidence, both died on the same day—July 4, 1826, the anniversary of the Declaration of Independence both had helped to write.

Adams was ninety years old at the time of his death. He and his wife, the remarkable Abigail Adams, were both buried at Braintree (now Quincy) Massachusetts, where his birthplace is still preserved. He had five children.

ROBERT TREAT PAINE

7TH SIGNER • MASSACHUSETTS

BORN: MARCH 11, 1731

BIRTHPLACE: BOSTON, MASS.

EDUCATION:
 HARVARD COLLEGE

OCCUPATION: LAWYER

MARRIED:
 SALLY COBB, 1770

AGE AT SIGNING: 45

DIED: MAY 11, 1814. AGE, 83

ROBERT Treat Paine was another of the Signers who could trace his ancestry back to the *Mayflower*. One of his ancestors had been a governor of Connecticut, and his father had been a minister until he gave up that calling to become a merchant.

Robert attended Harvard College and was educated for the ministry, but because of poor health he turned to the study of law instead. His political career began at the time of the Boston Massacre when he acted as associate prosecutor of the British soldiers charged with manslaughter. His vigorous speeches attacking the right of Britain to quarter soldiers on the colonists against their will attracted wide attention.

Paine was for five years a member of the colonial assembly in Massachusetts, and because of his reputation as a patriot was sent as a delegate to both the First and the Second Continental Congress. Here he became a close friend of John Hancock, though more moderate in his views. As one of those who still hoped for a peaceful settlement with England, he supported and signed the final "Olive Branch" petition in 1775. By 1776, however, he had become convinced of the necessity for complete independence. In fact, he was one of the few delegates who signed both the Olive Branch petition and the Declaration of Independence. He later became Washington's chief buyer of cannon.

Paine left the Congress in 1777 to become the first attorney general of Massachusetts, and several years later his friend Governor Hancock appointed him to the new supreme court of Massachusetts. In 1804, at the age of seventy-three, he retired to spend his last years in Boston.

In addition to his work as a lawyer and judge, Paine was deeply interested in the sciences, especially astronomy, and helped to found the American Academy of Arts and Sciences. He had been married in 1770 to Sally Cobb and had eight children.

ELBRIDGE GERRY

8TH SIGNER · MASSACHUSETTS

BORN: JULY 17, 1744

BIRTHPLACE:
MARBLEHEAD, MASS.

EDUCATION:
HARVARD COLLEGE

OCCUPATION: MERCHANT,
POLITICIAN

MARRIED:
ANN THOMPSON, 1786

AGE AT SIGNING: 32

DIED: NOV. 23, 1814. AGE, 70

ELBRIDGE Gerry, like his friend Samuel Adams, was an early and ardent advocate of independence from Great Britain. He was a native of Marblehead, Massachusetts, the son of an English shipowner who had settled there about 1730.

After graduating from Harvard College, Elbridge joined his father and brothers in the family business, but he also took a lively interest in public affairs. As a member of the Massachusetts legislature he met Samuel Adams, and under his influence Gerry soon became a fiery supporter of the revolutionary cause. He worked with Samuel Adams and John Hancock to gather arms and munitions for the patriots, and during the British march on Lexington and Concord he had to flee for his life into a cornfield, clad only in his nightshirt.

Early in 1776 Gerry was elected to the Second Continental Congress, where he became a close friend of both John Adams and Thomas Jefferson. He did valuable work in helping procure supplies and munitions for the army, and in July he voted for and later signed the Declaration.

Gerry continued to serve diligently in Congress after the Revolution, though his stubbornness and tendency to change his mind were unfortunate characteristics.

President John Adams appointed Gerry a member of a mission to France in 1797, but he quarreled with the other members because of his pro-French attitude. On his return, Gerry found himself out of favor with the Federalists but supported by the Republicans, who elected him governor of Massachusetts in 1810. The term "gerrymander" dates from this time and grew out of a redistricting bill Gerry supported which obviously benefited his own party. One district was so oddly shaped that it resembled a salamander, and angry Federalists coined the word "gerrymander" to describe it.

In 1812 Gerry was elected Vice President on the ticket with Madison, but two years later he died of a sudden seizure while on his way to the Senate. Although a controversial figure in his own time, Gerry nevertheless had the loyal support of John Adams, and is remembered as an honest and devoted patriot who did much to help arouse the revolutionary spirit in the colonies. "It is the duty of every citizen, though he have but one day to live, to devote that day to the service of his country," he said.

"GERRYMANDER."

STEPHEN HOPKINS

9TH SIGNER • RHODE ISLAND

BORN: MARCH 7, 1707

BIRTHPLACE: CRANSTON, R.I.

EDUCATION: SELF-TAUGHT

OCCUPATION: MERCHANT

MARRIED:
SARAH SCOTT, 1726
MRS. ANNE SMITH, 1775

AGE AT SIGNING: 69

DIED: JULY 13, 1785. AGE, 78

"MY HAND trembles, but my heart does not," said Stephen Hopkins, who suffered from palsy, as he signed the Declaration. Next to Franklin, Hopkins was the oldest of the signers. At the time of the signing of the Declaration, he was sixty-nine years old and one of the "elder statesmen" of the colonies. His family were among the original settlers of Rhode Island, and he had been active in local politics there for almost fifty years. The son of a farmer, he had only elementary schooling, but had educated himself by wide reading. He had served many terms in the Rhode Island legislature, and was nine times elected governor.

Even before 1760 Hopkins favored some plan of union for the colonies, and he and Benjamin Franklin became firm friends because of their similar views. In 1772, Hopkins was chief justice of Rhode Island at the time the revenue schooner *Gaspée* was seized and burned by a group of colonists as a protest against the Navigation Acts. The British government sent a commission to investigate and bring the culprits back to England for trial, but Hopkins, a "fighting Quaker," refused to have them arrested.

Hopkins was outspoken in his support of the cause of independence. At the First Continental Congress, when most of the delegates were advising caution, he said plainly: "Powder and shot will decide this question." As a delegate to the Second Congress, he signed the Declaration, and was appointed to the committee for drawing up plans for a navy. He also assisted in drawing up the Articles of Confederation.

In addition to his political activities, Hopkins took an interest in literary and scientific matters, was a member of the Philosophical Society of Newport, and the first chancellor of Rhode Island College, later to become Brown University. He married twice and had seven children. He died on July 13, 1785, at the age of seventy-eight, and was buried in Providence, Rhode Island.

WILLIAM ELLERY

10TH SIGNER • RHODE ISLAND

BORN: DEC. 22, 1727

BIRTHPLACE: NEWPORT, R.I.

EDUCATION:
HARVARD COLLEGE

OCCUPATION: MERCHANT, LAWYER

MARRIED:
ANN REMINGTON, 1750
ABIGAIL CARY, 1767

AGE AT SIGNING: 48

DIED: FEB. 15, 1820. AGE, 92

THE SECOND delegate from the tiny colony of Rhode Island was William Ellery, a lawyer and a native of Newport, where his grandfather had settled in the late seventeenth century.

After graduating from Harvard College, William Ellery tried his hand at various business enterprises, but finally became a lawyer. A sincere believer in the patriot cause, he was one of the leaders in local resistance to British rule, and was sent as a delegate to the Second Continental Congress, where he voted for and signed the Declaration. He was a witty and observant man, and is said to have placed himself so he could watch the faces of the other delegates as they signed the document. He reported later that they all showed "undaunted resolution."

Ellery continued as a member of the Congress, with one break of two years, until 1786, and served on many important government committees. After the organization of the government under the Federal Constitution (1789), Ellery was appointed by President Washington to the post of collector of customs for the Newport district. He

continued to hold this office until the time of his death in 1820, when he was ninety-two years old. He was next to the oldest of the Signers to die.

Ellery suffered very real losses in the Revolution as a result of his patriotic activities. When Newport was occupied by the British in 1776–77, his home was burned and many of his possessions were lost, but he later succeeded in rebuilding his fortunes. Always more of a man of letters than a politician, Ellery had a wide knowledge of literature and the classics and was a great letter writer. He was married twice—first to Ann Remington in 1750, and after her death, to Abigail Cary in 1767.

ROGER SHERMAN
11TH SIGNER · CONNECTICUT

BORN: APRIL 19, 1721

BIRTHPLACE: NEWTON, MASS.

EDUCATION: SELF-TAUGHT

OCCUPATION: LAWYER

MARRIED:
 ELIZABETH HARTWELL
 REBECCA PRESCOTT, 1763

AGE AT SIGNING: 55

DIED: JULY 23, 1793. AGE, 72

FIRST of the four Connecticut delegates to sign the Declaration, Roger Sherman was a self-made man, and a good example of what a shrewd, hard-working Yankee can accomplish. His father had been a farmer in Stonington, Massachusetts, and Roger received only a country-school education. Early in life, however, he acquired the habit of study, and read widely in many fields—particularly theology, law, and politics. His father taught him the shoemaking trade, and after his father's death Roger supported his mother and several younger children.

As a young man, he moved to New Milford, Connecticut, where an elder brother lived, and there he continued working as a shoemaker and also became a surveyor. He prospered in his work, held many local

offices, bought land, and then gave up shoe-making for the practice of law. Although self-taught, he soon became known for his shrewdness and legal ability. Sometime later he moved to New Haven, Connecticut, where he engaged successfully in various business ventures and also took part in public affairs.

For many years Sherman was both a member of the Connecticut legislature and a judge of the superior court. When the disputes began between the colonies and Great Britain, he was one of the first to challenge the authority of Parliament. Though not as radical in his views as some, he was head of the New Haven Committee of Correspondence, and also supported the non-importation agreements. He was a delegate to both the First and the Second Continental Congress, and was one of the five men appointed to draft the Declaration (see p. 11). John Adams called him ". . . an old Puritan, as honest as an Angel and as firm in the course of American Independence as Mount Atlas." Patrick Henry considered him one of the greatest statesmen he knew.

Because of his legislative experience, Sherman was one of the most influential figures in the Congress during the years of the Confederacy (1777–1789). He helped frame the Federal Constitution in 1787, and introduced the so-called "Connecticut Compromise" which provided for equal representation in the Senate and proportional representation in the House. After the new government was established, Sherman served first in the House of Representatives and then in the Senate. Always a conservative in his views, he believed in a strong central government and sound government finances.

Although not so colorful as some of the other colonial leaders, Sherman was a strong personality and an unswerving patriot. He held the distinction of being the only man to sign the Association of 1774, the Declaration of Independence in 1776, the Articles of Confederation in 1777, and the Federal Constitution in 1787. In his home town of New Haven he is still remembered. He married twice and had fifteen children.

SAMUEL HUNTINGTON
12TH SIGNER • CONNECTICUT

BORN: JULY 3, 1731

BIRTHPLACE:
  WINDHAM, CONN.

EDUCATION: SELF-TAUGHT

OCCUPATION: LAWYER

MARRIED:
  MARTHA DEVOTION, 1761

AGE AT SIGNING: 45

DIED: JAN. 5, 1796. AGE, 64

IN MANY details, Samuel Huntington's early life resembled that of Roger Sherman. He too was of Puritan ancestry, and his father was a farmer. He too had little schooling, but read widely and taught himself law, and then became active in public affairs in Norwich, where he had made his home. As a boy he was apprenticed to a cooper, but apparently he never worked at the trade. Like Sherman, he was a member of the Connecticut legislature and a judge of the superior court; for a time (1765) he was also the king's attorney for Connecticut.

Because he was known as an outspoken patriot, Huntington was selected as one of the Connecticut delegates for the Second Continental Congress, where he voted for and signed the Declaration. He continued as a member of the Congress for ten years, and for two years acted as its president. In 1786 he was elected governor of Connecticut and held this office for twelve years, which indicates that he was both liked and trusted by his fellow citizens. He even received two electoral votes for the Presidency in 1789—the first election held under the new Federal Constitution. This was probably in recognition of the strong support he had given the Constitution in Connecticut.

Huntington had a handsome home in Norwich, Connecticut, but like Sherman, he lived with Puritan simplicity and economy.

He was married to Martha Devotion in 1761, but the couple had no children. They did, however, adopt and bring up two of his brother's children, and one of these boys later became the governor of Ohio. Huntington died in 1796 at the age of sixty-four, and was buried in Norwich.

WILLIAM WILLIAMS

13TH SIGNER · CONNECTICUT

BORN: APRIL 8, 1731

BIRTHPLACE: LEBANON, CONN.

EDUCATION:
HARVARD COLLEGE

OCCUPATION: MERCHANT

MARRIED:
MARY TRUMBULL, 1771

AGE AT SIGNING: 45

DIED: AUG. 2, 1811, AGE, 80

WILLIAM Williams was a patriot and a Signer who literally gave his fortune to help the cause of independence. His family were of Welsh ancestry and had settled in Roxbury, Massachusetts, in the 1630's, so he belonged to one of the oldest colonial families. Both his father and grandfather were ministers in the Congregational church, and William Williams was born in Lebanon, Connecticut.

William attend Harvard College and then studied for the ministry under his father. When the French and Indian Wars began, however, he joined the colonial forces in 1755 and took part in the fighting around Lake George. After his return home he abandoned theology to become a merchant, and also began to take part in local politics. He was elected to the Connecticut legislature in 1757, and after serving there for nineteen years was sent as a delegate to the Second Continental Congress.

A man of strong feelings, Williams gave his whole-hearted support to the cause for independence, never hesitating when either his efforts or his money was required. In 1775 he signed promissory notes to raise money for the campaign against Ticonderoga, and in 1779, when the Continental currency was losing value, he exchanged his own gold and silver for paper money that soon became worthless. In 1780–81 he moved out of his house in Lebanon so that it could be used by the officers of a French regiment.

Williams continued active in public service all his life. He helped to frame the Articles of Confederation in 1777, and eleven years later was a member of his state convention which ratified the Federal Constitution. He was a member of the governor's council in Connecticut for twenty years.

Williams' wife was Mary Trumbull, the daughter of the governor of Connecticut. The couple made their home in Lebanon, Connecticut, where Williams died in 1811 at the age of eighty. He had three children.

OLIVER WOLCOTT
14TH SIGNER • CONNECTICUT

BORN: NOV. 20, 1726

BIRTHPLACE:
WINDSOR, CONN.

EDUCATION: YALE COLLEGE

OCCUPATION: LAWYER,
POLITICIAN

MARRIED:
LAURA COLLINS, 1755

AGE AT SIGNING: 49

DIED: DEC. 1, 1797. AGE, 71

O LIVER Wolcott, whose father had been a colonial governor of Connecticut, was the youngest in a family of fifteen children. Even as a youth he showed his leadership abilities. At Yale College he stood at the head of his class for four years, and before he graduated he received a captain's commission in the militia. He went directly from college to take part in a military expedition against Canada.

On his return he studied medicine for a time, but gave this up in favor of a career in law and politics. Wolcott was a member of the Connecticut legislature continuously from 1771 to 1786, and was also a county judge and a colonel in the militia. He was elected to both the First and the Second Continental Congress and took part in the debates on the Declaration. Ill health caused

him to leave Philadelphia in June, 1776, so that he was not present to vote for the Declaration. However, he showed his feelings by bringing home from New York a statue of George III, which was patriotically melted down for bullets in Wolcott's back yard. He later returned to Philadelphia and signed the Declaration in October.

During the war years Wolcott was constantly active in military affairs, first as a brigadier of militia and later as a major general, and took part in a number of campaigns in New York and Connecticut. In 1779 he was put in charge of defending the Connecticut seacoast against the British.

After the war, he served the new state of Connecticut first as lieutenant governor and then as governor, and he was holding the office of governor when he died in 1797.

Wolcott is described as being tall, dark complexioned, and dignified in appearance, and as energetic and strong-willed in character. A sturdy Puritan, he was known for his personal integrity, and as a firm believer in republicanism. He had five children.

WILLIAM FLOYD
15TH SIGNER • NEW YORK

BORN: DEC. 17, 1734

BIRTHPLACE:
BROOKHAVEN, L.I.

EDUCATION: AT HOME

OCCUPATION: LANDOWNER

MARRIED:
ISABELLA JONES
JOANNA STRONG

AGE AT SIGNING: 41

DIED: AUG. 4, 1821. AGE, 86

W ILLIAM Floyd, the 15th Signer, came from a long-established Long Island family. His father was a well-to-do landowner of Welsh descent, and William took over the management of the family estate upon his death. He was apparently educated at home.

By the time of the Continental Congresses, William Floyd had won a reputation as a leader in community affairs, and was a major general in the militia of his county. Ignoring the risks to his personal fortune, he boldly cast his lot with the colonial cause and was elected to both the First and the Second Continental Congress. Here he was respected as a committeeman of sound common sense, though he rarely took part in debates. Like other members of the New York delegation, he was not able to vote for the Declaration, but he did sign it later.

During the British occupation of Long Island in 1776, Floyd's home was twice attacked. The first time he was able to defend it; but the second time he and his family were forced to flee to Connecticut and suffered severe hardships. When the war ended, Floyd found himself almost ruined financially, but he continued his public services. He was a member of the first United States Congress (1789–91), and also served in the New York state senate.

In 1803, at the age of sixty-nine, Floyd and his family moved to a tract of land he had purchased in upstate New York, and here he took up the hard life of a pioneer. His first wife, Isabella Jones, had died in 1781, and he later married Joanna Strong, who became the mother of five children. Apparently he prospered, for he continued to live at this farm until his death in 1821.

PHILIP LIVINGSTON

16TH SIGNER • NEW YORK

BORN: JAN. 15, 1716

BIRTHPLACE: ALBANY, N.Y.

EDUCATION. YALE COLLEGE

OCCUPATION: MERCHANT

MARRIED:
CHRISTINA TEN BROECK

AGE AT SIGNING: 60

DIED: JUNE 12, 1778. AGE, 62

LIKE John Hancock of Massachusetts, Philip Livingston was a man of wealth and social position who took up the cause of liberty at the risk of great financial loss.

Livingston was the son of a wealthy landowner of Albany, New York, and was brought up almost like a young prince on a great estate. He was educated at Yale, and then went into the importing business in New York, where he soon became one of the most successful merchants in the city. At the time the Revolution was in its opening stages, he was very actively engaged in civic affairs. He was one of the founders of the New York Chamber of Commerce; he campaigned for the establishment of King's College (later Columbia), and was president of the St. Andrew's Society, the earliest benevolent institution in New York.

Politically, Livingston was a conservative patriot. He strongly opposed the Stamp Tax, and as a member of the Stamp Act Congress helped draft the protests against it, yet he was just as strongly opposed to acts of violence on the part of the colonists. He was a forceful opponent of the Intolerable Acts, but as a member of the First and Second Continental Congresses he argued against breaking away from England. He belonged to the conservative group who hoped to solve the colonial problems without actually asserting independence.

Since the New York delegation did not vote on the Declaration on July 4, it is not known what Livingston's position might have been, but he signed the document in August and thereafter supported it loyally. In retaliation, the British seized his lands. He continued as a member of the Congress, serving conscientiously on various committees, and also gave a large part of his personal fortune to help maintain the credit of the Continental Congress during the first hard years of the Revolution. He died while attending a session of the Congress at York, Pennsylvania, in 1778.

Livingston had married Christina Ten Broeck, a descendant of one of the old patrician Dutch families of New York, and the couple had a family of eight children. He founded a professorship in divinity at Yale College which still bears his name.

FRANCIS LEWIS

17TH SIGNER • NEW YORK

BORN: MARCH 21, 1713

BIRTHPLACE: LLANDAFF, WALES

EDUCATION: WESTMINSTER SCHOOL, LONDON

OCCUPATION: MERCHANT

MARRIED: ELIZABETH ANNESLEY, 1745

AGE AT SIGNING: 63

DIED: DEC. 31, 1802. AGE, 89

FRANCIS Lewis was born in Wales, the son of a clergyman, and was left an orphan as a young boy. However, his uncle, who was the Dean of St. Paul's in London, saw that he received an education and then apparently started him upon a business career. He came to New York when about twenty-five years old to begin a career as a merchant, and during the next twenty years or so built up a considerable fortune. These were years of adventure too, for twice

he was shipwrecked on voyages between the colonies and European ports, and in 1756, during the French and Indian Wars, he was captured by the Indians and sent to France for exchange.

In 1765, Lewis was able to retire from business, and from then on he devoted himself to public affairs. This was, of course, the time of the Stamp Tax agitation, and Lewis was soon taking an active part in the anti-British protests. He was unswerving in his support for the revolutionary party, and he showed the strength of his feelings by resigning from one committee because he thought the members too cautious in their attitude toward Britain.

As a delegate to the Second Continental Congress, Lewis worked tirelessly on a number of important committees, especially those dealing with supplies for the army, and with foreign affairs. He was a reticent man, but respected for his common sense and his business experience. The New York delegation could not vote on the Declaration of Independence because of instructions from the state legislature, but Lewis signed the document in August of 1776.

He and his family suffered heavily for their part in the Revolution. In September, 1776, his estate on Long Island was burned by the British, and his wife was taken prisoner. The hardships of her captivity hastened her death, and Lewis never succeeded in rebuilding his fortunes. He continued to serve in the Congress until 1781, but then retired from public life to live with some of his children. He was nearly ninety years old when he died in 1802.

LEWIS MORRIS

18TH SIGNER • NEW YORK

BORN: APRIL 8, 1726

BIRTHPLACE:
"MORRISANIA," N.Y.

EDUCATION: YALE COLLEGE

OCCUPATION: LANDOWNER

MARRIED:
MARY WALTON, 1749

AGE AT SIGNING: 50

DIED: JAN. 22, 1798. AGE, 71

LEWIS Morris, like Philip Livingston, was a member of the wealthy landowning aristocracy of New York. His grandfather had been the first royal governor of New Jersey, and Lewis inherited a large estate called "Morrisania" in Westchester County. He was graduated from Yale College, and in 1749 married the equally aristocratic and wealthy Mary Walton. They had ten children.

Morris was an early supporter of the pa-

triot cause, in spite of the disapproval of many of his patrician neighbors, who were inclined to be Tories. As a member of the New York provincial assembly he condemned British policy, and was sent as a delegate to the Second Continental Congress in 1775. In June of 1776 he was recalled to Westchester County to take command of the militia there, and so was not in Philadelphia when the debates on the Declaration of Independence took place. But after the Declaration was finally approved by the New York provincial congress, he signed the document later in the year.

During the war, Morris's rich estates were plundered and burned by the British, and after independence was won he devoted most of his time to restoring them. He did take part in local politics, however, was elected a member of the state legislature, and played an active part in gaining New York's ratification of the Federal Constitution.

Tall, handsome, and courtly in manner, Morris was also brave and generous in spirit and showed the best qualities of the colonial aristocrat. There can be no doubt that the association with the Morris name did much to add prestige to the colonial cause. He died at the age of seventy-one, and was buried with military honors at the family estate of "Morrisania."

RICHARD STOCKTON

19TH SIGNER • NEW JERSEY

BORN: OCT. 1, 1730

BIRTHPLACE:
STOCKTON MANOR, N.J.

EDUCATION: COLLEGE OF
NEW JERSEY

OCCUPATION: LAWYER

MARRIED:
ANNIS BOUDINOT

AGE AT SIGNING: 45

DIED: FEB. 28, 1781. AGE, 50

PERHAPS more than any other Signer, Richard Stockton underwent great personal suffering for his devotion to the cause of liberty. His fortune was sacrificed and his life shortened as a result of his patriotic stand in signing the Declaration of Independence.

Stockton was born near Princeton, New Jersey, where his father had a large estate. After graduating from the College of New Jersey (later to become Princeton College), he studied law, and within ten years had built up a very successful practice. At first Stockton had no interest in politics, but after a trip to Scotland in 1766 to persuade John Witherspoon to become president of the College of New Jersey, he found himself drawn into public affairs. He was appointed to the governor's council, and was also made a justice of the supreme court in New Jersey. His interest in Princeton College, of which he was a trustee, continued throughout his life.

In the disputes between Britain and the colonies, Stockton at first took a moderate position. He believed that Parliament had no authority over the colonies, but argued that some form of self-government would solve the difficulties. But when New Jersey ousted its royal governor in June of 1776 and elected five new members for the Continental Congress, Stockton was one of those chosen. He arrived in Philadelphia in June of 1776 and so heard the dramatic debate on the Declaration of Independence. Apparently his sympathies were now entirely with the patriot cause, for he signed the Declaration and later declined the position of chief justice in New Jersey to remain in the Continental Congress.

In the fall of 1776, when on a government mission to inspect the northern army, Stockton learned that New Jersey had been overrun by the British and that his family was in danger. He managed to get his family away from Princeton to safety, but was then betrayed and taken prisoner. Because of his known loyalty to the colonial cause he was treated with great severity, and when Congress finally arranged for his exchange, he found his home destroyed and his estate ruined. He never fully regained his health, and died an invalid at the age of fifty.

Stockton and his wife, the poetess Annis Boudinot, had six children, one of whom (Richard) became a prominent Federalist lawyer. Their daughter, Julia, married Dr. Benjamin Rush, a Signer from Pennsylvania (see p. 43).

JOHN WITHERSPOON

20TH SIGNER · NEW JERSEY

BORN: FEB. 5, 1723

BIRTHPLACE:
GIFFORD, SCOTLAND

EDUCATION:
UNIVERSITY OF EDINBURGH

OCCUPATION: CLERGYMAN

MARRIED:
ELIZABETH MONTGOMERY
MRS. ANN DILL, 1791

AGE AT SIGNING: 53

DIED: NOV. 15, 1794. AGE, 71

JOHN Witherspoon, a Presbyterian minister, was not only the only active clergyman in Congress but was one of the most prominent men in the colonies. Scotland born and educated, Witherspoon came to New Jersey at the urging of Richard Stockton and Benjamin Rush, fellow Signers, to become president of the College of New Jersey at Princeton.

During the years before (and after) the Revolution, John Witherspoon devoted himself to the development of Princeton and to the unification of the Presbyterian Church in America. He began to take an active interest in the colonial cause in 1774 and contributed to the cause of independence through his forceful sermons, debates, pamphlets, and essays. In June, 1776, as a member of the provincial congress of New Jersey, Witherspoon was the leader of a movement to oust the royal governor. As a result, he and four companions—called "the five independent souls" by John Adams—were sent as delegates to the Second Continental Congress. Since Princeton was disrupted by the war, Witherspoon could give his full efforts to public affairs.

At the Congress Witherspoon played an influential part in convincing delegates not to delay but to go forward. In the debates on the Declaration he asserted that the colonies were "not only ripe for the measure, but in danger of rotting for the want of it." He remained in the Congress until 1782, where his courage, patience, and grave dignity made him an impressive figure. He took part in the debates on the Articles of Confederation, helped to organize the new government, and fought for a sound currency. He also served on two important committees —the board of war and the committee on secret correspondence (foreign affairs).

Witherspoon devoted most of the later years of his life to rebuilding Princeton College and making it an intellectual center. He was also on the state legislature for a time. His first wife, Elizabeth Montgomery, who came with him from Scotland, bore him ten children, one of whom was killed while serving with the Continental Army. After Elizabeth's death, he married Mrs. Ann Dill in 1791. Three years later, at the age of seventy-one, John Witherspoon died. He was buried in the President's Lot at Princeton University, which he had done so much to create.

FRANCIS
HOPKINSON

21ST SIGNER • NEW JERSEY

BORN: OCT. 2, 1737

BIRTHPLACE:
PHILADELPHIA, PA.

EDUCATION: COLLEGE
OF PHILADELPHIA

OCCUPATION: LAWYER,
COMPOSER

MARRIED: ANN BORDEN

AGE AT SIGNING: 38

DIED: MAY 9, 1791. AGE, 53

IN ADDITION to being a Signer of the Declaration of Independence, Francis Hopkinson is remembered as the man who designed the first official American flag. He was a man of many talents—a musician and composer, a poet and an artist, something of an inventor, and also a lawyer. He is described as being small in stature but lively in manner and quick of speech.

Hopkinson was born in Philadelphia of English parentage. His father was a prominent lawyer, a member of the governor's council, and one of the founders of the American Philosophical Society. Francis was the first graduate of the first class of the College of Philadelphia. He then studied law, and was admitted to the bar in 1761. At the same time he was composing music and writing verse, and on a trip to England he studied drawing under Benjamin West, the foremost American artist of the time.

In 1768 Hopkinson married Ann Borden and settled in Bordentown, New Jersey, where he became a successful lawyer and was appointed to the governor's council. In the conflict with Great Britain, his sympathies from the first were with the colonial cause, and he wrote lively satirical articles about the British which attracted much applause. Elected to the Second Continental Congress, he was one of those who voted for and signed the Declaration.

Hopkinson continued to serve in the Congress throughout the war years, acting as chairman of the Continental Navy board from 1776–78, and as treasurer of loans from 1778–81. In 1777, when the Congress voted to adopt an official flag of thirteen stripes, alternate red and white, and a field of blue with white stars, it was Hopkinson who drew the actual design. Before this time the various colonies had devised flags of their own, but there had been no one flag for the whole nation. He also designed the seals for various government departments, as well as the Great Seal of New Jersey.

During these years Hopkinson was also active with his pen, encouraging the colonists and ridiculing the British. In 1781 he composed a cantata in honor of the French alliance. After the war, Washington appointed him a United States judge for Pennsylvania.

This versatile patriot was an intimate friend of both Benjamin Franklin and Thomas Jefferson, and was a member of the American Philosophical Society. He also took an active part in organizing the Protestant Episcopal Church in America.

The latter years of his life Hopkinson spent in Philadelphia; his home in Bordentown was looted by the British during the war. His family consisted of five children, and the eldest, Joseph, was the author of the popular patriotic song, "Hail, Columbia."

Hopkinson died suddenly in 1791, at the age of fifty-three.

JOHN HART
22ND SIGNER • NEW JERSEY

BORN: 1711

BIRTHPLACE:
  STONINGTON, CONN.

EDUCATION: SELF-TAUGHT

OCCUPATION: FARMER

MARRIED:
  DEBORAH SCUDDER, 1740

AGE AT SIGNING: 65

DIED: MAY 11, 1779. AGE, 68

ABRAHAM CLARK
23RD SIGNER • NEW JERSEY

BORN: FEB. 15, 1726

BIRTHPLACE:
  ELIZABETHTOWN, N.J.

EDUCATION: SELF-TAUGHT

OCCUPATION: LAWYER,
  FARMER

MARRIED:
  SARAH HATFIELD, 1749

AGE AT SIGNING: 50

DIED: SEPT. 15, 1794. AGE, 68

JOHN Hart was a "plain, honest, well-meaning Jersey farmer" who came to the Continental Congress after service in the New Jersey assembly. He was born in Stonington, Connecticut, had little schooling, but became a successful farmer and built up a considerable estate. As a leading citizen in his community, he was elected to the New Jersey legislature and held a seat there for ten years.

A believer in the rights of the colonists, Hart opposed the Stamp Act in 1765, and led the opposition in New Jersey against supplying provisions for British troops. In 1775 he was made a member of both the Committee of Safety and the Committee of Correspondence for his county, and in 1776 was elected to the Second Continental Congress. Shortly afterwards he was also chosen speaker for the newly formed state assembly of New Jersey.

Hart suffered great losses as a result of his loyalty to the patriot cause. Early in the war his lands and his mill property were laid waste by the British when they invaded New Jersey, his wife died, and he himself was forced to live as a fugitive in the forest. As a result of his privations and sufferings at this time his health failed; he died less than three years after the Declaration, and two years before independence was won.

In 1865 the New Jersey legislature, in memory of Hart's patriotic services, erected a monument to him in Hopewell, his home.

ABRAHAM Clark was another of those plain, self-educated patriots who in spite of little schooling served their country well. He was born and raised in Elizabethtown, New Jersey, where his father was an alderman. He was a frail boy and apparently his parents did not send him to school, but through his own efforts he taught himself the fundamentals of mathematics and law. He became a surveyor, a real estate dealer, and a general legal advisor, though he was never formally admitted to the bar. He was often critical of the methods of the legal profession, and because of his willingness to give advice free to the poor, he became known as the "Poor Man's Counsellor."

Clark held several local offices under the royal government, but because of his sympathy for popular rights he was attracted to the patriot party and soon became known as a champion of independence. In 1774 he became a member of the New Jersey Committee of Safety and was sent as a delegate to the Second Continental Congress where he voted for and signed the Declaration.

Clark's devotion to public service continued for the rest of his life, in spite of poor health. He was active in New Jersey politics and was a member of the convention that framed the state constitution in 1775. In 1787, when the new Federal Constitution was being debated, he was one of those who refused to approve it until a Bill of Rights was included.

Clark had married Sarah Hatfield in 1749, and the couple had ten children. His lifelong bitterness toward British rule was no doubt increased by the fact that two of his sons, on service with the Continental Army, were captured by the British and suffered severely before they were released.

Abraham Clark died of a sunstroke on September 15, 1794, when he was sixty-eight years old, and he was buried in Rahway, New Jersey.

ROBERT MORRIS

24TH SIGNER • PENNSYLVANIA

BORN: JAN. 31, 1734

BIRTHPLACE:
LIVERPOOL, ENGLAND

EDUCATION:
COMMON SCHOOLS

OCCUPATION: MERCHANT

MARRIED:
MARY WHITE, 1769

AGE AT SIGNING: 42

DIED: MAY 8, 1806. AGE, 72

R OBERT Morris, called the "financier of the Revolution," was one of the wealthiest men in the colonies, yet this did not prevent him from joining the fight for independence. He gave willingly of his wealth to finance the Continental Army and the struggling new government.

Morris was English by birth, the son of a well-to-do merchant in Liverpool. His father brought him to America while he was still a boy, and he grew up in Maryland. After attending school in Philadelphia for a time, he was placed in the home of a Philadelphia merchant to learn the business. While still a young man he became a partner in the firm, and then went on to amass a fortune.

Like other colonial merchants, Morris opposed the Stamp Tax because of its effect on trade. He supported the non-importation agreements and was an active member of the Committee of Safety in Philadelphia, but he took a cautious and conservative attitude toward actually declaring independence. As a Pennsylvania delegate to the Second Continental Congress, he argued that the colonies should not take action hastily on such an important step. He stayed away from Philadelphia on July 2, when the vote on the Virginia Resolution took place, but he accepted the decision of Congress and added his signature to the Declaration in August.

Morris showed his devotion to the patriot cause in very practical ways. He advanced money from his personal funds to buy supplies for Washington's army, and he often used his influence to borrow money when the government could not. In the Continental Congress he served on the committee on finance, and was also on the committee on secret correspondence, which worked with American agents in foreign countries. Later he was accused of making a profit out of these transactions, but many of his own ships were lost in the course of the war.

In 1781 Morris was appointed superintendent of finance, a very difficult position.

The war with England had drained the treasury, and the new nation was deeply in debt. Morris, through his financial skill, kept the government afloat, but he was bitterly criticized as a "dictator," and left office a discouraged man. However, he was elected to the convention of 1787 that framed the Constitution, and he strongly supported it. President Washington, who trusted and respected him, offered Morris the position of Secretary of the Treasury in his first Cabinet, but he declined this to become a United States Senator from Pennsylvania.

Morris's last years were tragic for a man who had served his country so well. He engaged in land speculations which collapsed and left him ruined; in 1798 he was arrested for debt and spent over three years in prison. After his release he lived in retirement in Philadelphia until his death in 1806. He and his wife had seven children.

BENJAMIN RUSH
25TH SIGNER • PENNSYLVANIA

BORN: DEC. 24, 1745

BIRTHPLACE: "BYBERRY," PA.

EDUCATION:
PRINCETON COLLEGE
AND UNIVERSITY
OF EDINBURGH

OCCUPATION: PHYSICIAN

MARRIED:
JULIA STOCKTON, 1776

AGE AT SIGNING: 30

DIED: APRIL 19, 1813. AGE, 67

BENJAMIN Rush, who was only thirty years old when he signed the Declaration, was the youngest of the Philadelphia delegation; he was also to become one of the most famous of American physicians.

Rush was born near Philadelphia and educated at Princeton (then the College of New Jersey), where he studied medicine. He continued his medical studies in Edinburgh and London, and then returned to Philadelphia in 1769. He soon attracted attention by his unusual ability, and within a few years was well established in his profession.

A man of wide sympathies and a quick and lively mind, Rush became enthusiastic about the colonial cause and was one of the Pennsylvania delegates to the Second Continental Congress. He took his place in July, 1776, too late to cast a vote for the Declaration, but he signed it with great satisfaction. In the Congress he formed close friendships with John Adams and Thomas Jefferson, both of whom he admired greatly. He had married earlier in this same year the daughter of Richard Stockton of New Jersey, another of the Signers (see p. 38).

Rush served briefly as the surgeon general for Washington's forces in 1777, but resigned because of a disagreement with Congress over the conduct of military hospitals. After this he threw himself into his medical work, both as a doctor and a teacher, and became widely known. When an epidemic of the dreaded yellow fever broke out in Philadelphia in 1793, Rush showed true heroism by remaining in the stricken city to care for the sick and dying. He established the first free dispensary in Philadelphia, was a member of the staff of the Pennsylvania Hospital, and also a founder of Dickinson College. He also worked energetically for many causes for the public good—such as campaigns against slavery, liquor, and capital punishment.

Rush also kept up his interest and activities in public affairs. He helped frame Pennsylvania's new state constitution and strongly supported the new Federal Constitution. In 1797 John Adams, then President, appointed Dr. Rush to the position of treasurer of the U. S. Mint, and he held this position until his death, in addition to his professional duties. Rush kept up his friendship with both Adams and Jefferson, and when these two old friends quarreled over political beliefs, it was Rush who finally brought about a reconciliation.

At the time of his death in 1813, Dr. Rush was sixty-seven years old and at the peak of his career. He and his wife had a family of thirteen children.

BENJAMIN FRANKLIN

26TH SIGNER • PENNSYLVANIA

BORN: JAN. 17, 1706

BIRTHPLACE: BOSTON, MASS.

EDUCATION: SELF-TAUGHT

OCCUPATION: PRINTER, STATESMAN, SCIENTIST

MARRIED: DEBORAH READ, 1730

AGE AT SIGNING: 70

DIED: APRIL 17, 1790. AGE, 84

BENJAMIN Franklin was the oldest and the most eminent Signer of the Declaration, a man of extraordinary talents and achievements. Jefferson called him "the greatest man and ornament of the age and country in which he lived." He was honored for his intellectual achievements, and beloved for his kindliness and humanity.

Franklin was born in Boston, the youngest son of Josiah Franklin, a soap- and candle-maker. His parents wanted him to become a minister, but since they lacked the money to educate him, he was apprenticed to his half-brother, a printer, instead. Franklin stayed with this brother for five years, learning the printing trade, and then at the age of seventeen left Boston to seek his fortune in Philadelphia.

Although Franklin's schooling was meager, he made himself one of the best-educated men in the colonies by a strict program of reading, writing, and self-discipline. In this way he learned grammar and logic, algebra and geometry, the principles of science, and the fundamentals of Latin, French, German, and Italian. In 1730, when he was twenty-four years old, he became the sole owner of a printing business, and in that same year he married Deborah Read, the daughter of his landlady. They had two children.

In addition to his printing business, Franklin also published the *Pennsylvania Gazette,* which he made into one of the most successful newspapers in the colonies. In 1732 he began publication of *Poor Richard's Almanack,* which became even more successful. The *Almanack* was filled with homey verses, witty sayings, and commonsense maxims which were quoted throughout the colonies and made "Poor Richard" a household word.

Franklin also took an interest in civic affairs in Philadelphia. In 1737 he became postmaster, and brought about so many improvements that the British government made him deputy postmaster general for all the colonies. At forty-two, Franklin virtually retired from business to devote himself to "philosophical studies and amusements." During the following years he carried out his famous scientific experiments with electricity, and also studied and charted the Gulf Stream and worked out a number of useful inventions, such as bifocal glasses.

The outbreak of the French and Indian War in 1754 led Franklin to propose a plan of union for the colonies, but because of colonial jealousies the plan failed. Beginning about 1757, Franklin spent many years in England where he acted as spokesman for the colonial cause and tried unavailingly to work out some plan of compromise with the British government. But when all at-

tempts at reconciliation failed, Franklin returned home in 1775, convinced that "Rebellion to tyrants is obedience to God." He
attended the Second Continental Congress,
where he drew up a plan of union and
served on many committees, including the
one that drafted the Declaration. Jefferson
no doubt used some of his suggestions.

In 1776 Franklin was sent to France to
draw up a treaty of alliance. During his
years there he became a hero to the French
people, and used his influence to gain valuable financial aid for the colonies. When the
war ended, he was a member of the committee that negotiated the treaty of peace
with Great Britain.

Franklin returned to Philadelphia in 1785,
but two years later he was again called on
to take part in the Constitutional Convention. Here his patience, humor, and wisdom
were immensely helpful in smoothing out
differences between the delegates. He was
especially concerned with working out the
"Great Compromise," which settled the dispute about representation in Congress.

Three years later, at the age of eighty-
four, Benjamin Franklin died. His last public act was to sign an appeal to Congress
for the abolition of slavery. He was buried
next to his wife, and half the population of
Philadelphia paid homage at his funeral.

JOHN MORTON

27TH SIGNER • PENNSYLVANIA

BORN: c. 1724

BIRTHPLACE: RIDLEY, PA.

EDUCATION: AT HOME

OCCUPATION:
SURVEYOR, FARMER

MARRIED:
ANN JUSTIS, 1754

AGE AT SIGNING: c. 52

DIED: APRIL, 1777. AGE, c. 53

ALTHOUGH John Morton was a delegate to both the First and the Second
Continental Congress, the records of his life
and activities are rather scanty. He was a
descendant of Swedish immigrants who had
settled as farmers on the Delaware River
near Philadelphia. His father died before
his birth, and his mother then married an
Englishman, John Sketchley, who was a
farmer and surveyor. Sketchley was well-
educated and taught his stepson at home,
giving him a good grounding in mathematics and other subjects.

John Morton entered public life early,
serving as a sheriff, justice of the peace, and

then as a member of the Pennsylvania provincial assembly. Later (in 1774) he became an associate judge on the Pennsylvania supreme court.

Evidently John Morton shared the anti-British feelings of the more extreme patriots, for he was a member of the Stamp Act Congress in 1765 and was a delegate to both Continental Congresses. As a member of the Pennsylvania delegation to the Second Continental Congress, he joined Franklin and James Wilson in voting for independence, in spite of the anger and disapproval of some of his more conservative friends.

Morton was the first of the Signers to die, falling ill of a fever in the spring of 1777. As he was dying, he said that he felt that the signing of the Declaration was "the most glorious service I have ever rendered my country."

He was survived by his wife and eight children. Today, in Philadelphia, a museum called the John Morton Memorial Building has been erected in his memory.

GEORGE CLYMER

28TH SIGNER • PENNSYLVANIA

BORN: MARCH 16, 1739

BIRTHPLACE:
PHILADELPHIA, PA.

EDUCATION: AT HOME

OCCUPATION: MERCHANT

MARRIED:
ELIZABETH MEREDITH

AGE AT SIGNING: 37

DIED: JAN. 24, 1813. AGE, 73

ALTHOUGH not so well known as some of the other Signers, George Clymer was a patriot who had been active in the cause of independence from his youth. He was the son of an Englishman who had settled in Philadelphia, but after the death of his parents he was brought up by his uncle, who was a wealthy merchant.

Like his uncle, George Clymer became a merchant, and he was later made a partner in the firm of Merediths and Clymer. He married Elizabeth Meredith, the daughter of the senior partner, in 1765. George Washington was a friend of the Merediths, and Clymer formed a friendship with him at their home. He was a quiet, modest man, but always well informed, and sincere.

As a firm believer in republican principles, Clymer showed an early interest in the revolutionary movement. He was a leader in the protest actions against the Stamp Tax in Philadelphia, and later served on the local Committee of Safety. In July, 1776, he was elected to the Second Continental Congress (together with several others) to replace some of the more conservative Pennsylvania delegates who were not willing to vote for independence. As a pledge of his patriotism, he exchanged all his money for Continental currency—thus risking ruin if the colonists were defeated. Though he did not have an opportunity to vote for the Declaration, he realized his "dearest wish" in signing it.

Clymer served in the Congress for several years, though not continuously, and was a hard and conscientious worker. He went on a mission to Ticonderoga in 1776 and to Fort Pitt (now Pittsburgh) in 1777–78, and he was also a member of the board of war and of the treasury board. Later he was elected to the Pennsylvania legislature.

Like many other Signers, Clymer suffered personal losses during the war when his home was ransacked by the British troops after the Battle of the Brandywine. He took part in the Constitutional Convention of 1787, and was elected to the First Congress. After negotiating a treaty with the Cherokee and Creek Indians in 1796, he retired.

Clymer was interested in cultural activities as well as politics, and was one of the founders and the first president of the Philadelphia Academy of Fine Arts. He died in Morrisville, Pennsylvania, at the age of seventy-three, but was buried in Trenton, New Jersey. His gravestone there states that he signed the Constitution, but does not mention the Declaration of Independence.

JAMES SMITH
29TH SIGNER • PENNSYLVANIA

BORN: 1719

BIRTHPLACE: IRELAND

EDUCATION:
  PHILADELPHIA ACADEMY

OCCUPATION: LAWYER,
  MANUFACTURER

MARRIED: ELEANOR ARMOR

AGE AT SIGNING: 57

DIED: JULY-11, 1806. AGE, 87

WE HAVE only a few details of the life of James Smith, the 29th Signer, since all his personal records were destroyed in a fire. He was Irish by birth, the son of an enterprising farmer who settled in York County, Pennsylvania, about 1729. Apparently he prospered, for James attended an academy in Philadelphia, then studied law, and passed the bar examinations. After living for four or five years on the Pennsylvania frontier, he began to practice law, but had so few clients that he turned to business instead, and set up an iron foundry.

Like most men of the frontier, Smith was a man of strong republican convictions, and thus opposed to British policy. Beginning about 1774, he served in the Pennsylvania legislature, where he urged the non-importation of British goods and helped draft resolutions calling for independence and the improvement of provincial defenses. He put his beliefs into practice by organizing and drilling a volunteer militia company in York. This later grew to a battalion, and he was made an honorary colonel.

Smith was one of the five new delegates elected by the Pennsylvania legislature to the Continental Congress in July of 1776. The Declaration had already been voted at that time, but he was present to sign it in August. He continued in the Congress until 1778, serving on various committees, and was noted for his sharp wit and lively conversation. Later he was appointed a judge in the Pennsylvania court of appeals, and was a member of the convention that drafted the state constitution. Although re-elected to Congress in 1785, he declined on account of his age. During his later years he continued to practice law, but did not take an active part in public life. He died in 1806.

GEORGE TAYLOR

30TH SIGNER • PENNSYLVANIA

BORN: 1716

BIRTHPLACE: IRELAND

EDUCATION:
NO INFORMATION

OCCUPATION: IRONMASTER

MARRIED:
MRS. ANNE SAVAGE, 1742

AGE AT SIGNING: 60

DIED: FEB. 23, 1781. AGE, 65

JAMES WILSON

31ST SIGNER • PENNSYLVANIA

BORN: SEPT. 14, 1742

BIRTHPLACE:
CARSKERDO, SCOTLAND

EDUCATION: UNIVERSITIES
OF ST. ANDREWS,
GLASGOW, EDINBURGH

OCCUPATION: LAWYER

MARRIED:
RACHEL BIRD, 1771
HANNAH GRAY, 1793

AGE AT SIGNING: 33

DIED: AUG. 21, 1798. AGE, 55

LIKE James Smith, George Taylor was born in Ireland, and like him, too, left few personal records. He was the son of a clergyman, and emigrated to Philadelphia in 1736, when he was about twenty years old. Having ambition but no money, he became a clerk in the office of an iron manufacturer, and when his employer died he took charge of the business. Later he married his employer's widow, Mrs. Anne Savage, and thus came into possession of the property. Some years afterward they seem to have made their home in Easton, Pennsylvania.

Taylor became active, though not prominent, in local politics, and served in the Pennsylvania provincial assembly for several years. As a western "radical," he was opposed to British colonial policy, and he was especially aroused by the "Intolerable Acts" of 1774. It was probably at that time that he became one of the patriot party favoring independence. His growing reputation as one of the radical patriots is shown by the fact that he was one of the five new Pennsylvania delegates sent to Congress in July of 1776 to replace more conservative members. He signed the Declaration in August.

After serving for less than a year in Congress, Taylor withdrew to serve on the Pennsylvania executive council, but because of ill health he gave up this office too and returned to the town of Easton, where he died in 1781. His wife had died in 1768, and neither of his two children survived him.

JAMES Wilson, the 31st Signer, was one of the most learned men in the Continental Congress. He was born in Scotland, and studied at the universities of St. Andrews, Glasgow, and Edinburgh. When in his early twenties he emigrated to America, settled in Philadelphia, and studied law under John Dickinson, a leader of the moderate party in colonial politics. In 1770 he moved to Carlisle, Pennsylvania, married Miss Rachel Bird, and soon built up a profitable law practice. Eventually, however, he made his home in Philadelphia.

Wilson was one of the first to take a definite stand denying the authority of Parliament over the colonies, and he wrote a pamphlet on this subject that had wide influence. As a delegate to the Second Continental Congress in 1775 he at first, like Dickinson, advised delay in making a break with England, but in the voting that took place on July 2, 1776, he cast his vote for the Declaration of Independence.

Wilson continued as a member of the Congress until the latter part of 1777, and was an impressive and influential figure there. Dr. Rush greatly admired his mental powers and his eloquence in debate. However, as time passed, Wilson became increasingly conservative in his views and lost the support of the public. In fact, his opposition to the popular democratic state constitution of Pennsylvania brought about a mob attack on him.

GEORGE ROSS

32ND SIGNER · PENNSYLVANIA

BORN: MAY 10, 1730

BIRTHPLACE:
NEW CASTLE, DEL.

EDUCATION: AT HOME

OCCUPATION:
LAWYER, JURIST

MARRIED:
ANNE LAWLER, 1751

AGE AT SIGNING: 46

DIED: JULY 14, 1779. AGE, 49

After the close of the war, the conservatives came back into power in Pennsylvania and Wilson was re-elected to Congress. He played a very influential part in the Constitutional Convention of 1787 and was on the committee that drafted the Constitution. Probably no other member except James Madison had a better grasp of the problems of setting up a constitutional government. Because of his legal ability he was appointed one of the first associate justices of the United States Supreme Court, and he was also a professor of law at the College of Philadelphia (later the University of Pennsylvania) He was on the committee that prepared the draft of the Federal Constitution, and later was one of the signers. After the death of his first wife he married the nineteen-year-old Hannah Gray in 1793.

Wilson continued to serve on the Supreme Court with distinction until some unfortunate land speculations caused his financial ruin. The shock of this failure, and the hostility of his creditors, brought about a mental and physical collapse, and he died at Edenton, North Carolina, when he was only fifty-five years old. Over a hundred years later his remains were taken to Philadelphia and reburied in Christ Church Churchyard.

A PORTRAIT of George Ross in his legal robes shows him as an attractive young man, and he is described as being handsome, good-humored, and popular. His ancestors were Scottish, and he was born in New Castle, Delaware, the son of a clergyman. Although he did not attend college he evidently received a good preparatory education, perhaps at home, and then studied law under his brother.

Ross was admitted to the bar in 1750, and then began to practice in Lancaster, Pennsylvania, where he became both successful and popular. It is said that one of his first clients was the lady he married—Anne Lawler. He was a member of the Pennsylvania legislature for many years, and was an attorney for the British government before he was won over to the patriot cause.

In 1774 Ross was elected to the First Continental Congress, where at first his sympathies were with the conservatives, or Loyalists, in opposing any break with England. By the next year, however, his opinions had completely changed and he now became an active supporter of the patriot cause. He was a tireless worker at the Pennsylvania state constitutional convention in 1776, helped draft the Pennsylvania "Declaration of Rights," and was elected to the Second Continental Congress in July of that year. Thus, like Taylor and Smith, he did not vote for the Declaration but he did sign it in August.

Ross took little active part in the later work of the Congress, although he was actively interested in Indian problems. In 1776 he helped negotiate a treaty of peace with the Indians of northwestern Pennsylvania. He resigned in 1777 because of illness and thereafter devoted himself to his legal work. According to one story that has come down to us, Congress voted him 150 pounds sterling in appreciation of his patriotic services, but he refused the gift, saying that what he did was for love of freedom and country. He was appointed judge of the admiralty court in Pennsylvania, but held the office only a short time, as he died in 1779. His family consisted of three children.

CAESAR RODNEY

33RD SIGNER • DELAWARE

BORN: OCT. 7, 1728

BIRTHPLACE: DOVER, DEL.

EDUCATION: AT HOME

OCCUPATION: LANDOWNER

AGE AT SIGNING: 47

DIED: JUNE 26, 1784. AGE, 55

THE STORY of how Caesar Rodney rode eighty miles through a storm to cast his vote for the Virginia Resolution on July 2, 1776, is one of the most dramatic incidents of that eventful day. It was his vote that broke the tie of the Delaware delegates.

As the son of a prosperous plantation owner in Delaware, young Caesar Rodney grew up in comfortable surroundings. He was educated at home, as the sons of planters often were, and held many local public offices while still a young man. He served in the Delaware provincial legislature for a number of years, and joined in the protests against the Stamp Tax in 1765 as a delegate to the Stamp Act Congress. Later, after the Townshend Acts, he was on the committee instructed by the Delaware assembly to draw up an address of protest to the king. He was also active in organizing militia groups, and in 1775 held the rank of a brigadier general.

Rodney was a delegate to both the First and the Second Continental Congress, and was a strong advocate for independence. It happened, though, that during the first days of July, 1776, he had returned to his own county to investigate a Tory uprising. Of the two other delegates from Delaware, Thomas McKean was in favor of the Virginia Resolution and George Read was against it, so Rodney's vote would decide which way the colony would go. McKean sent word to him to return to Philadelphia at once, and in spite of a severe storm and his own ill health he rode all night to reach Philadelphia on the morning of July 2, just in time to cast his vote. A plaque picturing the scene shows him striding into the meeting room still booted and spurred.

Rodney's service in Congress was brief, though it had been decisive. In spite of a painful and incurable disease, he later took an active part in securing recruits and provisions for Washington's army, and was appointed a major general of the militia in Delaware. During 1778–81 he was governor or "president" of Delaware, and continued to serve in the state legislature until his death in 1784.

John Adams described Rodney as being "tall, thin, and slender as a reed, pale; his face is not bigger than a large apple, yet there is sense and fire, spirit, wit and humor in his countenance." He never married. He was buried on his home farm, but a century later his remains were moved to the Christ Church burial ground in Dover. An equestrian statue of Rodney was erected in Wilmington in 1923, and there is also a statue of him in the Statuary Hall of the Capitol in Washington, D.C.

GEORGE READ

34TH SIGNER • DELAWARE

BORN: SEPT. 18, 1733

BIRTHPLACE:
CECIL COUNTY, MD.

EDUCATION:
PHILADELPHIA ACADEMY

OCCUPATION: LAWYER

MARRIED:
GERTRUDE ROSS TILL, 1763

AGE AT SIGNING: 42

DIED: SEPT. 21, 1798. AGE, 65

GEORGE Read, the 34th Signer, was a patriot of Irish descent and was born in Maryland, the son of a well-to-do landowner there. After studying law in Philadelphia, he moved to New Castle and became a prominent lawyer in the "Three Lower Counties," as Delaware was called before statehood. The Three Lower Counties had the same governor as Pennsylvania, but a separate legislative body. These counties wanted independence and separation from Pennsylvania as much as from Great Britain, and this was achieved in 1776. They then took the name of Delaware.

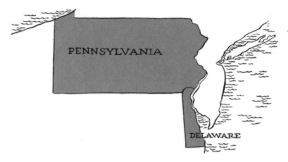

Read had been a member of the provincial assembly of the Three Lower Counties for many years before he was sent as a delegate to the Continental Congress. He strongly protested the Stamp Act and fought hard to bring about non-importation agreements, but he took a cautious view of the movement for complete independence. In fact, as a delegate to the Second Continental Congress, he at first opposed the Declaration of Independence (see p. 12), but he later signed it and supported it staunchly.

In addition to his work at the Congress, Read took a leading part in the Delaware state constitutional convention of 1776, and was active in writing the state constitution. When the newly elected president (or governor) of the state was captured by the British, Read (as vice president) took his place, and by his energy and example roused the citizens to new efforts.

Read was always a champion of the smaller states and fought to protect their interests. He objected to some of the provisions in the Articles of Confederation but nevertheless supported it, since he recognized the need for some form of union. Later, as a delegate to the Constitutional Convention of 1787, he strove to provide safeguards for the small states. He favored a strong central government to prevent the large states from getting too much power. Largely due to his efforts, Delaware was the first state to ratify the Constitution.

Read was elected a United States Senator from Delaware but resigned in 1795 to become chief justice of his state, and he held this office until his death in 1798. He had married Gertrude Ross Till, a widow and the sister of George Ross. They had five children.

THOMAS McKEAN

35TH SIGNER • DELAWARE

BORN: MARCH 19, 1734

BIRTHPLACE: NEW LONDON
TOWNSHIP, PA.

EDUCATION:
PHILADELPHIA ACADEMY

OCCUPATION:
LAWYER, JUDGE

MARRIED:
MARY BORDEN, 1763
SARAH ARMITAGE, 1774

AGE AT SIGNING: 42

DIED: JUNE 24, 1817. AGE, 83

THOMAS McKean's career spread over two states, Delaware and Pennsylvania, and he was probably the only Signer to hold political offices in two states at the same time. This was possible because Delaware, before 1776, was considered a part of Pennsylvania. (See p. 51.)

Born in Pennsylvania, he was educated there and in Delaware, and then practiced law. His career in politics began early. He was appointed a deputy attorney general in 1756, and was a member of the Delaware assembly for seventeen years. When the Stamp Act was passed, he immediately attacked it, and as a justice of the court of common pleas, refused to use the stamps on legal documents in his court.

McKean was one of the most active patriots in calling for a Colonial congress in 1774, and as a delegate became one of the most urgent in advising complete independence from Britain. When the Declaration of Independence was being debated in July, 1776, it was McKean who summoned Caesar Rodney to Philadelphia to break the tie in the Delaware delegation (see p. 50). Later in 1776 McKean was active in drafting Delaware's state constitution, and was elected speaker of the Delaware assembly. But he was also becoming more and more involved with Pennsylvania politics (he had moved to Philadelphia in 1774), and while still serving in the Delaware assembly he was appointed chief justice for Pennsylvania, a

position he held for twenty-two years. Until 1783 he also represented Delaware at the Continental Congress, where he energetically supported the Articles of Confederation and attacked corruption and inefficiency. He also worked to secure the ratification of the Federal Constitution in 1787.

Although McKean leaned toward the Federalists in his belief in a strong central government, he was elected governor of Pennsylvania by the Republicans in 1799. As governor, he came into conflict with the more extreme radicals who were constantly attacking the state constitution, and his administration was a stormy one. His policy of removing his political opponents from office aroused much criticism, but on the whole he was a man of honesty and ability who did much to restrain the radical element.

McKean remained in Philadelphia after his retirement from office, and died at the age of eighty-three. He was twice married and had eleven children, but only four survived him.

SAMUEL CHASE

36TH SIGNER • MARYLAND

BORN: APRIL 17, 1741

BIRTHPLACE:
SOMERSET COUNTY, MD.

EDUCATION: AT HOME

OCCUPATION: LAWYER

MARRIED:
ANNE BALDWIN, 1762
HANNAH KILTY GILES, 1784

AGE AT SIGNING: 35

DIED: JUNE 19, 1811. AGE, 70

SAMUEL Chase was Maryland's fieriest patriot. He was one of the first to rise against the British when, as a member of the provincial assembly, he sided with the faction opposing the proprietary governor. (In Maryland, as in Pennsylvania and New

Jersey, the governor represented the Proprietor rather than the Crown.) He violently opposed the Stamp Act, and was a member of the radical "Sons of Liberty." The mayor of Annapolis denounced him as an "inflaming son of discord."

Chase was the son of an Episcopalian clergyman who had emigrated to Maryland from England. He was tutored at home by his father, then studied law, and had built up a very successful practice in Annapolis before 1765. From the beginning of the disputes with England, he was a leader in the radical wing of the patriot party and was violently anti-British.

Chase was a delegate to both Continental Congresses, and almost single-handedly brought Maryland to support the Declaration of Independence. Revolutionary sentiment had never been strong in Maryland, but Chase put on such a vigorous campaign that the provincial assembly finally ordered its delegates to vote for independence. Chase then made the long ride to Philadelphia (150 miles in two days) with the fresh instructions, arriving on July 1, just a day before the final vote was taken.

During the next two years Chase continued as a member of the Congress, and served on as many as thirty committees. About this time, however, his career was clouded by scandal. His business dealings were criticized and Maryland dropped him

as a delegate; in 1789 he became bankrupt. However, he continued practicing law and in 1791 was appointed chief justice of the general court in Maryland. In 1796, President Washington appointed Chase an associate justice of the Supreme Court, and in this position he made some very important and far-reaching decisions. Unfortunately, his high-handedness and intense partisanship led to his impeachment in 1805. Though acquitted, his later career was unimportant.

Chase is described as a big, red-faced man, whose nickname was "Bacon Face." One colleague said that he had "more learning than knowledge, and more of both than judgment." But though radical in his opinions and aggressive in action, the enthusiasm and vitality of his devotion to the cause of independence were invaluable during the Revolution and the early years of the new nation. He was seventy years of age when he died (of gout) in 1811. He had four children.

WILLIAM PACA

37TH SIGNER • MARYLAND

BORN: OCT. 31, 1740

BIRTHPLACE: ABINGDON, MD.

EDUCATION: COLLEGE OF
   PHILADELPHIA,
   INNER TEMPLE, LONDON

OCCUPATION:
   LAWYER, JURIST

MARRIED:
   MARY CHEW, 1763
   ANNE HARRISON, 1777

AGE AT SIGNING: 35

DIED: OCT. 13, 1799. AGE, 58

WILLIAM Paca came of a family of wealthy Maryland planters who were probably of Italian origin. He attended the College of Philadelphia, and then studied law at Annapolis and at the Inner Temple in London.

When he returned to Maryland about 1762 he married, established a flourishing law practice in Annapolis, and at an early date committed himself to the revolutionary cause, although he was never one of the more violent patriots. As a member of the provincial assembly, however, he opposed the proprietary governor, and with Thomas Johnson and Samuel Chase wrote a series of articles against the poll tax in Maryland which attracted wide attention.

Paca was a member of both Continental Congresses and voted for and signed the Declaration of Independence. He was also a member of the Maryland Committee of Safety, and during the war spent thousands of dollars of his own money to outfit the American troops. He helped draft the first state constitution for Maryland and was a member of the first state senate.

After the war Paca served in various judicial offices and was elected governor of Maryland three times (1782–85). As governor, he showed special concern for the wel-

fare of returning soldiers, and worked hard to establish a peacetime society. He also encouraged the founding of Washington College, and laid the cornerstone for the first building. President Washington appointed him a United States district judge in 1789, and he lived out his remaining years in that capacity.

Paca died in 1799 at the age of fifty-eight, survived by his second wife and one child of his first marriage. His entire adult life was devoted to the young nation, and he was concerned in every significant political movement in Maryland during his lifetime.

THOMAS STONE
38TH SIGNER • MARYLAND

BORN: 1743

BIRTHPLACE:
CHARLES COUNTY, MD.

EDUCATION: AT HOME

OCCUPATION: LAWYER

MARRIED:
MARGARET BROWN, 1768

AGE AT SIGNING: 33

DIED: OCT. 5, 1787. AGE, 44

THOMAS Stone was the grandson of one of the early governors of Maryland, and was the youngest Signer from that colony. He was born at Poynton Manor in Charles County. After being admitted to the bar in 1764 he began to practice in the town of Frederick, married a few years later, and then moved back to Charles County where he bought land for a plantation.

In 1774, during the poll tax controversy in Maryland, Stone was one of the lawyers acting against the very patriots who were to be his colleagues only two years later. Actually, his sympathies were with the colonists, and he was elected to the Second Continental Congress in 1775. He was the most moderate member of the Maryland delegation, and wished to avoid war.

Although a steadfast patriot, Stone was quiet and inconspicuous. He rarely took part in debate, either in the Congress or in Maryland's senate, of which he was also a member. His most important service, in addition to voting for and signing the Declaration, was his work on the committee that drafted the Articles of Confederation in 1777. He also served one term in the Congress of the Confederation but declined reelection in order to resume his law practice.

He was elected to the Constitutional Convention of 1787, but did not attend because of his wife's failing health. When she died in June, 1787, he became ill with grief and died in October of the same year. Both are buried at their estate of "Habre de Venture" in Charles County, one of the most beautiful examples of colonial architecture in Maryland. Three children survived him.

CHARLES CARROLL

39TH SIGNER • MARYLAND

BORN: SEPT. 19, 1737

BIRTHPLACE: ANNAPOLIS, MD.

EDUCATION: CATHOLIC AND
    FOREIGN SCHOOLS

OCCUPATION: LANDOWNER

MARRIED:
    MARY DARNALL, 1768

AGE AT SIGNING: 38

DIED: NOV. 14, 1832. AGE, 95

CHARLES Carroll of Carrollton was not only the one Roman Catholic to sign the Declaration, but was also probably the wealthiest man in the colonies at that time. Carroll's grandfather, who claimed descent from the kings of Ireland, had emigrated to colonial Maryland and acquired large tracts of land there.

Charles Carroll was born into the aristocracy. He was educated by the Jesuits and had many years of schooling in Europe. After studying law in Paris and London, he returned to Maryland at the age of twenty-eight, and took over Carrollton Manor, the estate his father had given to him. This was in 1765, at the time of the Stamp Tax controversy, and Carroll soon associated himself with the colonial cause. His religion, however, prevented him from taking part in politics, since Catholics could not hold public office.

His entry into the political sphere came in 1773, when he wrote a series of articles supporting the cause of the colonists under the title of "First Citizen." These articles proved Carroll's standing as a patriot, and

he became known as the "First Citizen" of Maryland. In 1774–75 he took an active part in the work of Maryland's Committee of Correspondence and Committee of Safety, and also supported the non-importation agreements. Early in 1776 Carroll, Benjamin Franklin, and Samuel Chase went to Canada in an unsuccessful attempt to persuade the Canadians to join forces with the colonies. On their return, Carroll was elected to the Second Continental Congress. Like other delegates who arrived too late to vote for the Declaration in July, he nevertheless signed it in August. Carroll also had a hand in the framing of the Maryland state constitution, and supported the "Declaration of Rights" that insured religious freedom.

After the adoption of the Federal Constitution in 1787, Carroll served in both the United States Senate and in the Maryland state senate. Like most of the wealthy landowners who supported the cause of independence, he was a conservative politically.

In 1800, after a quarter of a century of public service, Charles Carroll retired to care for his 80,000-acre estate. He lived to see the beginning of the age of steam and the opening up of the western territories by the railroad. In fact, his last public appearance was when he laid the cornerstone for the Baltimore and Ohio Railroad in 1828. Four years later he died, at the age of

ninety-five, the last surviving Signer of the Declaration. He was buried in the chapel on the Carroll family estate.

GEORGE WYTHE

40TH SIGNER • VIRGINIA

BORN: 1726

BIRTHPLACE: ELIZABETH CITY COUNTY, VA.

EDUCATION: AT HOME

OCCUPATION: LAWYER, JURIST

MARRIED: ANN LEWIS, 1747 ELIZABETH TALIAFERRO

AGE AT SIGNING: 50

DIED: JUNE 8, 1806. AGE, 80

GEORGE Wythe was perhaps the foremost classical scholar in Virginia, and one of the most influential legal minds of his day.

His father was a prosperous plantation owner, and his mother came of Quaker stock. When Wythe was three years old his father died, and since the estate then passed to his elder brother, George and his mother were left in reduced circumstances. Margaret Wythe, an unusually well-educated woman, tutored her son in Latin and Greek and inspired in him a lifelong devotion to the classics. He later studied law with a family friend, and in 1747 married Ann Lewis, the sister of his legal associate. She died a year later, and for the next eight years Wythe apparently led a rather idle life.

Then in 1755 his elder brother died, leaving George the large family estate. Soon afterward he married Elizabeth Taliaferro and moved to Williamsburg, where he began to work and study in earnest. It can truly be said that his career began at the age of thirty. It was while Wythe was practicing law in Williamsburg that the young Jefferson studied under him. (See p. 58.)

Wythe was a member of the Virginia House of Burgesses for several sessions between 1758 and 1775. As a man of liberal views, he championed the cause of colonial rights, and at the time of the Stamp Tax controversy he drafted the Virginia "Resolutions of Remonstrance." In 1775 he was elected to the Continental Congress, where he staunchly supported Richard Henry Lee's resolution for independence.

After signing the Declaration, Wythe took a leading role in Virginia politics, and in 1778 he became a judge for Virginia's new high court of chancery. "Chancellor Wythe," as he was now called, began his most important work when he accepted the professorship of law at the College of William and Mary—the first chair of law in any American college. With his profound knowledge of the law and his penetrating mind, he did much to map the future course of American jurisprudence.

Wythe remained at William and Mary until 1790, when his duties moved him to Richmond. Here he founded a law school of his own, and became the teacher of many eminent students. He was honored and loved by his associates both for his learning and for his modesty and simplicity of character.

In 1806, when he was eighty years of age, Wythe died of the effects of poison given him by his grandnephew, who was his heir.

The grand-nephew was tried for murder, but could not be convicted because the only witness was the Negro cook, whose testimony was not admissible under Virginia law.

George Wythe's handsome brick home in Williamsburg has now been restored, and is visited by thousands of people yearly.

RICHARD HENRY LEE

41ST SIGNER · VIRGINIA

BORN: JAN. 20, 1732

BIRTHPLACE: WESTMORELAND COUNTY, VA.

EDUCATION: TUTORS, SCHOOLS IN ENGLAND

OCCUPATION: PLANTER

MARRIED:
ANNE AYLETT, 1757
ANNE GASKINS PINCKARD, 1769

AGE AT SIGNING: 44

DIED: JUNE 19, 1794. AGE, 62

AT THE time of the Second Continental Congress, Richard Henry Lee was the most prominent member of the illustrious Virginia delegation. Wealthy, distinguished, and well-educated both at home and abroad, Lee had served in the Virginia House of Burgesses and was a leader of the most aggressive wing of the patriot party. In appearance, he was tall and thin, with a rather stilted manner.

In the early days of the struggle with England, Lee had publicly denounced the Stamp Act, and was the author of Virginia's address to the king protesting against it. His Westmoreland Association, formed to boycott British goods, was the first of its kind in the colonies. With Jefferson and Patrick Henry, he helped found the Virginia Committee of Correspondence.

As a member of the First Continental Congress, Lee urged a policy of non-importation of British goods, and the Continental Association that was formed as a result was the first step toward a union of the colonies. Lee found in Samuel Adams a kindred spirit, and they became lifelong friends.

In the Second Continental Congress it was Lee who, as leading member of the Virginia delegation, proposed the famous resolution calling for a Declaration of Independence. He was the natural choice to compose the Declaration itself, but he was recalled to Virginia while the debate was still going on, and the task therefore fell to Thomas Jefferson. This was perhaps a happy circumstance, since Lee's talents were oratorical—he was known as the "Cicero of the Revolution"—while Jefferson was the superior writer.

After the signing of the Declaration, Lee's prominence waned. He strongly supported the Articles of Confederation and he was interested in foreign affairs, but unfortunately he became involved in some controversies which dimmed his popularity. However, he was a member of the Constitutional Convention of 1787, where he again showed his revolutionary spirit by opposing the Constitution because he feared the central government was being given too much power. His chief objections were that the first ten amendments—the "Bill of Rights"—should be added before ratification rather than after, and that they should precede rather than follow the main body of the Constitution. Lee was not elected to the ratifying conven-

tion in Virginia, but he afterward served in the United States Senate.

Lee died at his estate, "Chantilly," at the age of sixty-two. He had been married twice and had nine children.

THOMAS JEFFERSON
42ND SIGNER • VIRGINIA

BORN: APRIL 13, 1743

BIRTHPLACE: ALBEMARLE COUNTY, VA.

EDUCATION: COLLEGE OF WILLIAM AND MARY

MARRIED: MARTHA WAYLES SKELTON

OCCUPATION: LAWYER, PLANTER

AGE AT SIGNING: 33

DIED: JULY 4, 1826. AGE, 83

THOMAS Jefferson, the author of the Declaration of Independence and the supreme spokesman for liberty and democracy in American life, was the youngest member of the Virginia delegation. He had been elected as a substitute for Peyton Randolph of the Congress, whose presence was needed in Virginia.

Born into a distinguished Virginia family, Jefferson was graduated from the College of William and Mary, and studied law under George Wythe, later a fellow-Signer of the Declaration. He practiced law from 1767 to 1774 and during these years was also a member of the Virginia House of Burgesses. In 1772 he married a beautiful and wealthy young widow, Martha Wayles Skelton.

From the beginning of the trouble with Great Britain, Jefferson stood with his friend Patrick Henry and other outspoken champions of colonial rights. He helped draw up the resolution for the Virginia Committee of Correspondence, and proposed a day of fasting when the Boston Port Act went into effect. From the first he favored complete independence rather than any compromise

with Great Britain. Elected to the Continental Congress in 1775, he drew up several resolutions which were rejected as being too strongly worded and too anti-British in tone at that time.

In June of 1776 Jefferson was appointed to the committee that was to draft a Declaration of Independence, and by general consent was chosen to do the actual writing. In this document (see pp. 11–15) he set forth a brilliant summary of the revolutionary philosophy of the times.

Jefferson returned to Virginia in the fall of 1776 and spent the next three years in working out a far-reaching program to reform Virginia's code of laws. His bill for establishing religious freedom in Virginia was introduced at this time. After an unhappy term as governor of Virginia during the British invasion, Jefferson retired to his estates, but the loneliness caused by the death of his beloved wife in 1782 brought him back to public life. In 1784 he was appointed Minister to France to succeed Franklin, and remained abroad for five years.

In 1790 Washington appointed Jefferson his first Secretary of State, and later he became Vice President under John Adams, at that time a close friend. In 1800 he was elected President and served two terms. During his administration he brought about the purchase of the Louisiana Territory from France, sent the Lewis and Clark expedition across the Rocky Mountains, and kept America out of the Napoleonic wars. He became the leader of the Democratic Republicans, as opposed to the Federalists.

Jefferson lived out the later years of his life at his beautiful estate of "Monticello," where he busied himself with writing, with the encouragement of education in Virginia, and with many other interests ranging from architecture to music. His concern was always with human liberty, and he contributed a faith in the dignity of the common man to American life. Jefferson's achievements rank him as one of the greatest Americans, but he himself wished to be remembered for three works, which he directed to be listed on his tombstone:

Here was buried Thomas Jefferson/author of the Declaration of American Independence/of the Statute of Virginia for religious freedom/and Father of the University of Virginia.

He died on the same day as his old associate, John Adams—July 4, 1826—the anniversary of the Declaration of Independence. Only two of his six children survived him.

BENJAMIN HARRISON

43RD SIGNER · VIRGINIA

BORN: 1726(?)

BIRTHPLACE:
CHARLES CITY COUNTY, VA.

EDUCATION: COLLEGE OF
WILLIAM AND MARY

OCCUPATION: PLANTER

MARRIED:
ELIZABETH BASSETT, c. 1745

AGE AT SIGNING: 50

DIED: APRIL 24, 1791. AGE, 65

T HE BENJAMIN Harrison of Revolutionary fame is known as "the Signer" to distinguish him from other members of the family who had the same name. His ancestors had been among the earliest settlers in Virginia. Benjamin attended the College of William and Mary, but he left there on his father's death to take charge of the family plantation.

A member of the Virginia House of Burgesses for over twenty-five years, Harrison was often chosen as speaker of that body. When the controversy with England developed, he sided with the patriot party, and was a member of the committee which drew up a strong protest against the Stamp Act. He was a member of the Virginia Committee of Correspondence, and was elected to the First Continental Congress in 1774. His eagerness is shown by his statement—quoted by John Adams—that he would "come on foot rather than not come." He was naturally a delegate to the Second Congress.

Although he did not often take part in debates, Harrison played an important role in organizing the new government. He was on the committees for foreign affairs, marine affairs, and war and ordnance, and also served on a number of important committees dealing with finances. Washington, a fellow Virginian, relied on him confidently.

During the eventful months of 1776–77, Harrison was almost continually chairman of the "committee of the whole," and thus presided over the debates on the Declaration of Independence and later on the Articles of Confederation. His firmness and fairness made him an ideal presiding officer.

Late in 1777 Harrison returned to the Virginia legislature, and he also served three terms as governor. As governor, he showed an equal devotion to his state and to the Federal government he had helped to establish. Like Richard Henry Lee, he objected to the Constitution because he wanted to see the Bill of Rights given more prominence, but once it was accepted, he gave it his loyal support.

Benjamin Harrison, whose size and jovial personality won him the title of "the Falstaff of the Congress," was the father of William Henry Harrison, ninth President of the United States, and an ancestor of Benjamin Harrison, the twenty-third President. He died at sixty-five, after forty years of public service. He left seven children.

THOMAS NELSON
44TH SIGNER • VIRGINIA

BORN: DEC. 26, 1738

BIRTHPLACE: YORKTOWN, VA.

EDUCATION: CAMBRIDGE
    UNIVERSITY, ENGLAND

OCCUPATION: MERCHANT,
    PLANTER

MARRIED:
    LUCY GRYMES, 1762

AGE AT SIGNING: 37

DIED: JAN. 4, 1789. AGE, 50

THE 44th Signer of the Declaration was Thomas Nelson of Yorktown, Virginia, described by John Adams as "a fat man . . . alert and lively for his weight." Thomas was the son and grandson of well-to-do Virginia planters; his father had at one time been acting governor of the colony.

Although educated at Cambridge University in England, Nelson's sympathies were from the first with the colonists rather than with the British. One of his close friends was the young Thomas Jefferson, and possibly he was influenced by Jefferson's enthusiasm for democracy.

Under the colonial government Nelson was a member of the governor's council, like his father, but he soon showed that he believed in the cause of independence. He enthusiastically supported Patrick Henry's "call to arms" in 1775, and it was Nelson who carried the Virginia Resolution to the Second Continental Congress in 1776.

Nelson left the Congress in 1777 to take up military duties as a brigadier general in command of the Virginia militia. He succeeded Thomas Jefferson as governor in 1781, when the British were invading Virginia, and he joined Washington in the final siege of Yorktown. Cornwallis, the British commander, had established his headquarters in Nelson's house there, and according to tradition, Nelson directed the fire of the American batteries against his own home to drive the British out.

The war cost Nelson a great part of his fortune, for he had used his own money to fit out and provision troops during the Virginia campaign, and it also injured his health. After the war, he and his family moved to a small estate in Hanover County, where he died in 1789.

Nelson had eleven children. Among his descendants were Thomas Jefferson Page and Thomas Nelson Page, the novelist and diplomat.

FRANCIS LIGHTFOOT LEE

45TH SIGNER • VIRGINIA

BORN: OCT. 14, 1734

BIRTHPLACE: WESTMORELAND COUNTY, VA.

EDUCATION: AT HOME

OCCUPATION: PLANTER

MARRIED: REBECCA TAYLOE, 1769

AGE AT SIGNING: 41

DIED: JAN. 11, 1797. AGE, 62

CARTER BRAXTON

46TH SIGNER • VIRGINIA

BORN: SEPT. 10, 1736

BIRTHPLACE: KING AND QUEEN COUNTY, VA.

EDUCATION: COLLEGE OF WILLIAM AND MARY

OCCUPATION: PLANTER, MERCHANT

MARRIED:
JUDITH ROBINSON, 1755
ELIZABETH CORBIN, 1761

AGE AT SIGNING: 39

DIED: OCT. 10, 1797. AGE, 61

FRANCIS Lightfoot Lee was the younger brother of Richard Henry Lee, and like him was born at the family home of "Stratford" in Westmoreland County, Virginia. Apparently he received his education from tutors, and he became a member of the Virginia House of Burgesses when only twenty-four years old. Like his brother, he was deeply interested in politics, and was a devoted patriot. Perhaps he was even more revolutionary in his views than Richard, but because of his shy and retiring nature, he was never as well known. Still, he took an active part in all of the Virginia conventions defying Great Britain.

Francis was not a member of the original Virginia delegation to the Second Continental Congress, but joined it later when one of the older members resigned. Though he seldom engaged in debates, his sound judgment and fervent patriotism made him a valuable committee member. He retired from the Congress in 1779 but continued to serve as a member of the Virginia legislature. When the Federal Constitution was being drafted in 1787, he differed from his brother in strongly supporting the new form of government. He also showed farsighted wisdom in helping to secure free navigation of the Mississippi for Americans.

Francis spent his later years on his plantation "Menokin" in Richmond County, where he died in 1797. He left no children.

LIKE the other members of the Virginia delegation to the Second Continental Congress, Carter Braxton was a wealthy plantation owner. His parents had died when he was young, but he was educated at the College of William and Mary in Williamsburg and later, after the death of his first wife, spent several years in England. Perhaps as a result of these British contacts, he was more conservative in his views on independence than most of his fellow Virginians. However, he was an active member of the Virginia House of Burgesses for many years, was a member of the conventions in Virginia that favored revolution, and signed

the non-importation agreements. This was a pledge that meant real sacrifice on his part, since he was a merchant as well as a planter. In 1775 he was appointed a member of the Virginia Committee of Safety.

Braxton was elected to the Second Continental Congress early in 1776, and he was therefore in Philadelphia in time to vote for and to sign the Declaration. Later that same year he returned to Virginia, where he continued to serve as a member of the state legislature for most of his life. Although Braxton was a conservative in his views and did not favor a democratic form of government, he showed a more liberal spirit in supporting Jefferson's proposal for the establishment of religious freedom in Virginia.

Braxton married twice and had sixteen children. He suffered heavy financial losses during the war through loss of his cargoes and the failure of many men who owed him money. In his later years he moved from his spacious country estate, "Elsing Green," to Richmond, where he died in 1797.

WILLIAM HOOPER

47TH SIGNER · NORTH CAROLINA

BORN: JUNE 17, 1742

BIRTHPLACE: BOSTON, MASS.

EDUCATION: HARVARD
  COLLEGE

OCCUPATION: LAWYER

MARRIED:
  ANNE CLARK, 1767

AGE AT SIGNING: 34

DIED: OCT. 14, 1790. AGE, 48

WILLIAM Hooper, the 47th Signer, was a Bostonian by birth. He was the son of a Scotch Congregational minister who had emigrated to America after his marriage and settled in Boston. William attended Harvard College and then studied law under James Otis, one of the foremost

Massachusetts patriots, who had led the fight against the Stamp Tax in 1765. From him Hooper undoubtedly gained a sympathy for the colonial cause, in spite of the fact that his parents remained loyal to Britain.

After being admitted to the bar, Hooper moved to North Carolina where he settled in Wilmington and married the daughter of one of the prominent families there. He was attractive in appearance, with cultivated tastes and a gift for oratory, and soon became a successful lawyer. He was at one time the deputy attorney general, and as an officer of the royal government took part in a military expedition against the settlers on the western frontier who were agitating against the rule of the more aristocratic eastern counties.

In the conflicts with Great Britain, however, Hooper was solidly on the side of the colonists, and was sent as a delegate to both of the Continental Congresses. Revolutionary feeling was high in North Carolina; in fact, the provincial congress there voted for independence even before Virginia. Both John Adams and Dr. Rush were impressed with Hooper's ability in debate, and he was appointed to a number of important committees. He was absent from Philadelphia when the vote was taken on the Declaration, but signed it later.

In 1777 Hooper had to return to North Carolina because of business difficulties, but he continued his public services as a member of the state legislature. When the British captured Wilmington in 1781, he had to flee, leaving his family behind, and although they later rejoined him, his home was badly damaged. Later he settled in Hillsboro, North Carolina, and resumed his public services. He strongly supported the Federal Constitution, and although he did not have an opportunity to vote for it, he lived to see it ratified by North Carolina. After several years of declining health, he died in 1790. Some time later his remains were reburied in Guilford Courthouse National Military Park, and a monument was erected to him.

JOSEPH HEWES

48TH SIGNER • NORTH CAROLINA

BORN: JAN. 23, 1730

BIRTHPLACE: KINGSTON, N.J.

EDUCATION:
COMMON SCHOOLS

OCCUPATION: MERCHANT

AGE AT SIGNING: 46

DIED: NOV. 10, 1779. AGE, 49

ALTHOUGH Joseph Hewes was a member of the North Carolina delegation to the Second Continental Congress, he was born in New Jersey. His parents were Quakers who had settled on a farm near Kingston.

Joseph was apprenticed as a boy to a Philadelphia merchant after completing his schooling, and it was not long before he acquired a business of his own and a considerable fortune. Sometime before 1763 he moved to Edenton, North Carolina, where he set up a profitable shipping business. About this time he became engaged to a young lady, but she died before their wedding day, and Hewes never married.

Popular and respected in his community, Hewes was elected to the North Carolina

legislature in 1766 and continued as a member there until 1775. He was one of the leaders in the resistance movement against Great Britain from the start. Beginning in 1773, he was a member of the local Committee of Correspondence, and he was sent as a delegate to both the First and the Second Continental Congress. At the First Congress he helped prepare the "Declaration of Rights," and he supported the non-importation agreements in spite of their effect on his own shipping business.

But though Hewes was an enthusiastic patriot in defending the rights of the colonies, he did not at first favor an actual break with Great Britain. A peace-loving and friendly man, he hoped to avoid any violence. He wrote to an English friend: ". . . we want no revolution. But every American is determined to a man to die or to be free." At the Second Continental Congress he hesitated to vote for the Declaration until John Adams convinced him that this was the will of the people of his state.

Once he had given his vote, however, Hewes worked wholeheartedly for the American cause. Because of his knowledge of shipping he was made chairman of the marine committee, and with this authority he appointed his friend John Paul Jones to a command in the Continental Navy and found a ship for him. He is said to have ad-

vised Washington in planning the campaign of 1776, and he worked with such energy and concentration that he often went twelve hours at a time without food or drink.

As the result of such overwork his health broke down and he died after a brief collapse in 1779. He was buried in Christ Church Churchyard in Philadelphia, but a monument was later erected to him in Edenton, North Carolina, on the courthouse green.

JOHN PENN
49TH SIGNER • NORTH CAROLINA

BORN: MAY 6, 1740

BIRTHPLACE:
CAROLINA COUNTY, VA.

EDUCATION: SELF-TAUGHT

OCCUPATION: LAWYER

MARRIED:
SUSANNAH LYME, 1763

AGE AT SIGNING: 36

DIED: SEPT. 14, 1788. AGE, 48

JOHN Penn, though the son of a well-to-do farmer or planter in Virginia, had little formal schooling. His father made no effort to have him educated, and it was not until after the father's death that John received much encouragement to study. Then a relative, Edmund Pendleton, gave him the use of his own library to study law. He made the most of this opportunity, was admitted to the bar in 1761, and rapidly gained success and popularity.

In 1774 Penn and his wife moved from Virginia to Williamsboro, North Carolina, where some of his relatives were living. Penn was a likeable young man and soon became a leader of the patriot group in the community. He was elected to the provincial congress in 1775, and from there was sent as a delegate to the Second Continental Congress, together with Joseph Hewes and William Hooper.

Penn became convinced of the need for complete independence and urged his associates to "encourage and animate our people." In 1776 he returned to North Carolina to take part in the provincial congress that authorized support for such a declaration. Penn returned to Philadelphia in time to cast his vote for the Virginia Resolution, and later, of course, voted for and signed the Declaration.

Penn was a hard and conscientious worker in the Congress, remaining at his post there even though it meant considerable financial loss to him. He served almost continuously from 1775 to 1780, even declining a judgeship in 1777. In 1780 he returned to North Carolina and served briefly as a member of the board of war there at the time of the British invasion, but then returned to private life. Ill health prevented any further public duties, and he died in 1788 at the age of forty-eight. A monument to him and to William Hooper now stands at Guilford Battleground. He had three children.

EDWARD RUTLEDGE
50TH SIGNER • SOUTH CAROLINA

BORN: NOV. 23, 1749

BIRTHPLACE:
CHARLESTOWN, S.C.

EDUCATION:
MIDDLE TEMPLE, LONDON

OCCUPATION: LAWYER,
PLANTER

MARRIED:
HENRIETTA MIDDLETON,
1774
MARY EVELEIGH, 1792

AGE AT SIGNING: 26

DIED: JAN. 23, 1800. AGE, 50

THE YOUNGEST of all the Signers, Edward Rutledge was only twenty-six and a half years old when he voted for the Declaration in July of 1776. He was the younger brother of John Rutledge, who had been one of the leading spirits in the Stamp Act Congress in 1765, and who later played an important part in the history of South Carolina.

Edward was born in Charlestown (later Charleston), studied law under his distinguished brother and also in England, and then returned to Charleston in 1773 to practice. A year later he was elected to the First Continental Congress, where he gave vigorous support to the "Declaration of Rights," and also to the hopes of his brother that a reconciliation with England might still be possible.

The next year he returned to the Second Continental Congress as the leader of the South Carolina delegation. Because of his uncertainty about public opinion in South Carolina, he at first wished to postpone the decision on the Declaration, but when the time came for the vote in July, he decided that his delegation should join with the other colonies to make the vote unanimous.

Rutledge left Congress later in 1776 to take part in the defense of South Carolina as an officer in the militia. When the British attacked Charleston in 1780, he was captured and was imprisoned at St. Augustine, Florida, for a year before being exchanged.

After the close of the Revolution, Rutledge returned to his law practice in Charleston and won both honors and financial success. From 1782–98 he was a member of the South Carolina legislature, and as a Presidential elector in 1796 he voted for Jeffer-

son, although he was normally a staunch Federalist. In 1798 he was elected governor of the state. By this time, however, his health had failed and he died in 1800 before completing his term of office.

Rutledge married twice and had three children.

THOMAS HEYWARD, Jr.
51ST SIGNER · SOUTH CAROLINA

BORN: JULY 28, 1746

BIRTHPLACE:
ST. HELENA'S PARISH, S.C.

EDUCATION:
MIDDLE TEMPLE, LONDON

OCCUPATION: LAWYER

MARRIED:
ELIZABETH MATHEWES
SUSANNA SAVAGE, 1786

AGE AT SIGNING: 30

DIED: MARCH 6, 1809. AGE, 62

LIKE most of the delegates from the southern colonies, Thomas Heyward was the son of a wealthy plantation owner. After completing his elementary education at home, he was sent to England to study law in the Middle Temple, London, and re-

turned to South Carolina in 1771 when he was twenty-five years old. Two years later he married his first wife, Elizabeth Mathewes.

During his stay in England, Heyward had been angered by the contempt for the colonies he found there, and when he returned to South Carolina he at once became a supporter of the colonial cause. He was elected to the South Carolina assembly in 1772, and in 1774, after Parliament had closed the Port of Boston and passed the "Intolerable Acts," he took part in the provincial congresses called to protest this action. He became a member of the revolutionary Committee of Safety which practically took over the government of South Carolina, and in 1776 he was one of a committee of eleven appointed to prepare a state constitution. As one of the four South Carolina delegates to the Second Continental Congress, he voted for and signed the Declaration, and he continued to serve in the Congress until 1778. Benjamin Rush considered him a "firm republican."

Heyward returned to South Carolina in 1778 to become a circuit judge, but he was also a captain of artillery in the militia, and when the British invaded South Carolina he took part in the fighting at Port Royal Island in 1779 and in the defense of Charleston in 1780. During the Charleston campaign he was wounded and taken prisoner. Like Middleton and Rutledge, he was sent to the St. Augustine prison, where he stayed until exchanged in 1781. He then returned to Charleston and his duties as a circuit judge.

In 1785 Heyward helped to found the Agricultural Society of South Carolina, becoming its first president. He married his second wife, Susanna Savage, in 1786, and three years later resigned from his judgeship to give more time to the management of his plantation. He died in 1809 at the age of sixty-two, and was buried on his father's plantation. In 1920 a monument was erected over his grave by the state of South Carolina in recognition of his patriotic services during the Revolution.

THOMAS LYNCH, Jr.

52ND SIGNER • SOUTH CAROLINA

BORN: AUG. 5, 1749

BIRTHPLACE: PRINCE GEORGE'S PARISH, S.C.

EDUCATION: ETON AND CAMBRIDGE, ENGLAND

OCCUPATION: PLANTER

MARRIED: ELIZABETH SHUBRICK, 1772

AGE AT SIGNING: 26

DIED: 1779. AGE, 30

THOMAS LYNCH, the 52nd Signer, was elected to the Second Continental Congress as a substitute for his father, who had suffered a stroke of paralysis. Thomas was not quite twenty-seven at this time—and only a few months older than the youngest of the Signers, Edward Rutledge.

Thomas Lynch had grown up on his father's plantation in Prince George's Parish, South Carolina, and was then sent to England to complete his education. He attended Eton College, the famous preparatory school for boys, went on to Cambridge University, and then studied law in the Middle Temple. However, on his return to South Carolina in 1772, he persuaded his father to let him give up the law and become a planter.

With the encouragement of his father, who had been active in the colonial cause ever since the Stamp Act Congress, Thomas soon began to take part in public affairs. He was elected to many local offices, and was a member of the committee that drew up a new constitution for South Carolina. He was also elected a captain of the militia, and while on military service unfortunately fell ill with a fever which left him a semi-invalid for the rest of his life.

Thomas Lynch, Senior, had been elected as a delegate to both the First and the Second Continental Congress. When he fell ill early in 1776 his son was sent as an alternate delegate, and it was therefore Thomas Junior who voted for and signed the Declaration. Because of his own poor health, however, he was unable to take an active part in the work of the Congress, and later that year, father and son set out together for South Carolina.

Thomas Senior died on the way, and the son reached home in a very serious condition. After two more years of illness, he and his wife took a ship for the West Indies, intending to go from there to France. But the ship was never heard from again, and it was presumed wrecked with the loss of all lives. Thomas Lynch was the youngest, though not the first, of the Signers to die.

ARTHUR MIDDLETON

53RD SIGNER · SOUTH CAROLINA

BORN: JUNE 26, 1742

BIRTHPLACE: "MIDDLETON PLACE," S.C.

EDUCATION: AT HOME AND IN ENGLAND

OCCUPATION: PLANTER

MARRIED: MARY IZARD, 1764

AGE AT SIGNING: 34

DIED: JAN. 1, 1787. AGE, 44

LIKE the other three delegates from South Carolina, Arthur Middleton was the son of a wealthy plantation owner and studied law in England, yet returned to America to become a champion of colonial rights.

Arthur returned to South Carolina from England in 1763 and for the next several years was a member of the provincial assembly. A painting by Benjamin West indicates that he was a handsome youth, but he was said to have a violent temper. When the dispute over colonial rights was coming to crisis, Middleton became a leader of the ex-

treme wing of the patriot party. He took part in practically every action in South Carolina directed against the British. Briliant, generous, and public spirited, he was one of the most active patriots. He helped raise funds to support the colonial cause, was a member of the Council of Safety; urged preparations for the defense of Charleston, and was on the committee that drafted a new state constitution. Unlike his father, who was moderate in his views, Arthur Middleton proposed ruthless measures toward the British and their sympathizers. He did not even object to tarring and feathering the Tories.

In 1776 Middleton was elected to the Second Continental Congress to succeed his father, and voted for and later signed the Declaration. But when the British attacked the southern colonies he hastened home to aid in the defense of South Carolina and served with the militia during the siege of Charleston. Here he was captured by the British and spent a year in St. Augustine, Florida. After his release he returned to the

Continental Congress, and remained there until the close of the war in 1782.

Middleton then returned to South Carolina and devoted the rest of his life to restoring his estates, which had suffered considerably during the war. He lived the life of a wealthy and cultivated country gentleman, and showed his interest in intellectual affairs by becoming one of the original trustees of the College of Charleston. He had nine children.

He was only forty-four years old when he died in 1787. He was buried on the family plantation of "Middleton Place," which has become famous for its beautiful gardens.

BUTTON GWINNETT

54TH SIGNER · GEORGIA

BORN: 1735

BIRTHPLACE:
GLOUCESTERSHIRE, ENGLAND

EDUCATION:
COMMON SCHOOLS

OCCUPATION: MERCHANT,
PLANTER

MARRIED:
ANNE BOURNE, 1757

AGE AT SIGNING: 41

DIED: MAY 16, 1777. AGE, 42

NOT MUCH is known of the early life of Button Gwinnett except that he was born in England and that his father was a clergyman of Welsh descent. Apparently he attended the common schools, or perhaps was educated at home by his father. In 1757 he was married to Anne Bourne, and for the next few years was occupied as a merchant, exporting goods to the American colonies. This led to his emigrating to Georgia, and in 1765 he settled in Savannah. Shortly afterward he purchased a tract of land on St. Catherine's Island, just off the coast, and became a planter.

St. Catherine's Island was near Sunbury, the settlement of New Englanders where

Lyman Hall was the leading citizen (see p. 69). Gwinnett and Hall became close friends, and through this fellowship Button Gwinnett was drawn into politics as a supporter of the patriot party. He served briefly in the Georgia assembly, but he did not become really active until 1776, when he was elected as a delegate to the Second Continental Congress, together with Lyman Hall and George Walton. He was in Philadelphia during the debate on the Declaration and cast his vote for it, and signed it in August. He then returned to Georgia where he took an important part in drafting the new state constitution. In fact, he is said to have brought back a copy of the Pennsylvania constitution and used it as his model.

Button Gwinnett had hoped to be appointed to a military command in Georgia, and in 1777 he did achieve this ambition for a brief time when he was elected to succeed Governor Bullock. But as commander-in-chief of the Georgia forces, Gwinnett came into conflict with General Lachlan McIntosh. When a military expedition into Florida failed, an inquiry was held to see whether Gwinnett or McIntosh was to blame, and in the heat of the controversy the general called Gwinnett a scoundrel. Gwinnett promptly challenged him to a duel with pistols, and when they fought the next

morning, both men were wounded. Gwinnett died three days later.

At the time of his death Gwinnett was bankrupt, and it is not even known where he was buried. Because of the fact that he left so few written records, his signature has become remarkably valuable to collectors. Only fourteen known autographs of his exist, and in 1924 one of these was sold for a price of $14,000.

LYMAN HALL

55TH SIGNER · GEORGIA

BORN: APRIL 12, 1724

BIRTHPLACE: WALLINGFORD, CONN.

EDUCATION: YALE COLLEGE

OCCUPATION: PHYSICIAN

MARRIED:
ABIGAIL BURR, 1752
MARY OSBURN

AGE AT SIGNING: 52

DIED: OCT. 19, 1790. AGE, 66

LYMAN Hall, who came to Georgia from Connecticut, was one of the earliest and strongest spokesmen for the patriot cause in the southernmost colony.

He had been born in Wallingford, Connecticut, and was of Puritan ancestry. Lyman attended Yale College and then studied theology under an uncle, but apparently he was not well suited for the ministry. After quarreling with his first congregation for several years, he gave up preaching to study medicine.

About 1754 Hall left Wallingford, going first to South Carolina and then two years later to a settlement in Georgia called Sunbury. Dr. Hall, as a man of education and cultivated manners, soon became a leader here. He established a successful medical practice and also became a rice planter.

Georgia at this time was a sparsely settled frontier colony, and the settlers there still felt the need for the protection and support of England. Consequently they were largely Loyalist in feeling. Hall, as a New Englander, did his best to stir up revolutionary sentiment against England, and St. John's Parish, where he lived, became the headquarters of the patriot party. When the Georgia provincial congress failed to elect any delegates to the Continental Congress, Hall called an independent convention. This convention elected him as its delegate, and he accordingly attended the Second Continental Congress in 1775, although at first he was not allowed to vote. However, the next year Georgia elected him officially with two other delegates, and he was thus able to vote for and sign the Declaration.

Hall remained in Philadelphia as a member of the Congress until 1780. His home in Savannah and his rice plantation were destroyed by the British in 1778, and he then brought his family north for safety. After the end of the war, however, he returned to Georgia to make his home in Savannah, and in 1783 he was elected governor. He served only a brief term, but during that time he recommended that a tract of land be set aside for a state-supported college, and this led to the founding of Franklin College and the University of Georgia.

Hall died in 1790, just a few months after settling on a new plantation in Burke County. He had married twice but had only one child.

GEORGE WALTON

56TH SIGNER • GEORGIA

BORN: 1741

BIRTHPLACE: PRINCE EDWARD
COUNTY, VA.

EDUCATION: SELF-TAUGHT

OCCUPATION: LAWYER

MARRIED:
DOROTHY CAMBER, 1775

AGE AT SIGNING: 35

DIED: FEB. 2, 1804. AGE, 63

AMONG all the delegates from the southern colonies, George Walton is the only one who came from really poor beginnings. Little is known about his parents except their names. He was born in Virginia but was left an orphan at an early age and was then brought up by an uncle.

This uncle apprenticed George to a carpenter who, noting his intelligence and ambition, released him from his apprenticeship so he could attend school. Eager for an education, he read widely and was thus largely self-taught. About 1769 he moved to Savannah, Georgia, studied law, and was admitted to the bar five years later. Almost at once he became known as a fervent patriot. He drew up resolutions condemning the British, helped organize patriot groups in Savannah, was chosen secretary for the provincial congress summoned in 1775, and later was elected president of the Committee of Safety.

Early in 1776 he was elected a delegate to the Second Continental Congress and was re-elected almost continuously until 1781. He served on a number of important committees with zeal and intelligence. Like the other Georgia delegates, Walton re-turned to Georgia in 1778 when the British attacked the province, and served as a colonel in the militia during the siege of Savannah. Here he was wounded and captured by the British. When he was released, about a year later, the British were in control of Georgia and the patriot party was divided. Walton was elected governor by one faction, but after only two months in office he returned to the Continental Congress, where he remained until the end of the war.

In the years after the war, Walton devoted much of his time and energy to Georgia affairs. He served as chief justice for six years, and was elected governor in 1789. Later he served several terms as a judge of the superior court, and he was also one of the founders of Richmond Academy.

In spite of the fact that his manner was often stern and haughty and his temper apt to be violent, Walton was respected and

honored by the public. He was small in size but dignified in bearing, and equally warm in his likes and dislikes. His wife, Dorothy Camber, was the daughter of a British Loyalist, but she was as ardent in her support of the colonial cause as her husband. They had two sons.

Walton died in Augusta in 1804. A monument to him and Lyman Hall was erected there in 1848.

FACTS ABOUT THE SIGNERS

The Roster of The Thirteen Original Colonies and Their Signers

CONNECTICUT – 4
Roger Sherman
Samuel Huntington
William Williams
Oliver Wolcott

DELAWARE – 3
Caesar Rodney
George Read
Thomas McKean

GEORGIA – 3
Button Gwinnett
Lyman Hall
George Walton

MARYLAND –4
Samuel Chase
William Paca
Thomas Stone
Charles Carroll

MASSACHUSETTS – 5
John Hancock
Samuel Adams
John Adams
Robert Treat Paine
Elbridge Gerry

NEW HAMPSHIRE – 3
Josiah Bartlett
William Whipple
Matthew Thornton

NEW JERSEY – 5
Richard Stockton
John Witherspoon
Francis Hopkinson
John Hart
Abraham Clark

NEW YORK – 4
William Floyd
Philip Livingston
Francis Lewis
Lewis Morris

NORTH CAROLINA–3
William Hooper
Joseph Hewes
John Penn

PENNSYLVANIA – 9
Robert Morris
Benjamin Rush
Benjamin Franklin
John Morton
George Clymer
James Smith
George Taylor
James Wilson
George Ross

RHODE ISLAND–2
Stephen Hopkins
William Ellery

SOUTH CAROLINA – 4
Edward Rutledge
Thomas Heyward, Jr.
Thomas Lynch, Jr.
Arthur Middleton

VIRGINIA – 7
George Wythe
Richard Henry Lee
Thomas Jefferson
Benjamin Harrison
Thomas Nelson
Francis Lightfoot Lee
Carter Braxton

Nationalities of the Signers

Foreign born – 8
England – 2
Ireland – 3
Scotland – 2
Wales – 1

American born – 48
Connecticut – 5
Delaware – 2
Maryland – 5
Massachusetts – 10
New Jersey – 3
New York – 3
Pennsylvania – 5
Rhode Island – 2
South Carolina – 4
Virginia – 9

Occupations of the Signers

(Some Signers had more than one occupation.)

Lawyers – 23	Manufacturers – 2
Merchants – 12	Planters – 6
Farmers – 2	Landowners – 4
Doctors – 4	Printer – 1
Minister – 1	Politician – 1

Education of the Signers

Harvard College – 8
Yale College – 4
Princeton College – 2
College of William & Mary – 3
College (or Academy) of Philadelphia – 5
Foreign colleges – 10
Tutors, home – 9
Common schools – 6
Self-taught – 8
No information –1

Miscellaneous Facts

The youngest of the Signers:
Edward Rutledge, 26½ years
The oldest of the Signers:
Benjamin Franklin, 70 years
The first to die:
John Morton, April, 1777
The last to die:
Charles Carroll,
November 14, 1832

Ages of Signers at Death:

30–39 years – 1
40–49 years – 7
50–59 years – 10
60–69 years – 15
70–79 years – 9
80–89 years – 11
90–99 years – 3

"ALL eyes are opened to the rights of man . . . let the annual return of this day forever refresh our recollection of these rights, and an undiminished devotion to them."

THOMAS JEFFERSON
From his last letter, written June 24, 1826.

INDEX

ACKNOWLEDGMENT

Grateful acknowledgment is made to the Library of Congress for the series of engravings of the Signers of the Declaration used in this book, and also for facsimile of Jefferson's draft of the Declaration on p. 13, and the reproduction of the Declaration on p. 22.